The Great Queen Consort

BOOKS BY URSULA BLOOM

The House of Kent
The Duke of Windsor
Requesting the Pleasure
Princesses in Love
The Royal Baby
Life Is No Fairy Tale

The Great Queen Consort

URSULA BLOOM

ROBERT HALE · LONDON

First published in Great Britain 1976

ISBN 0 7091 5659 6

Robert Hale & Company
Clerkenwell House
45-47 Clerkenwell Green
London EC1

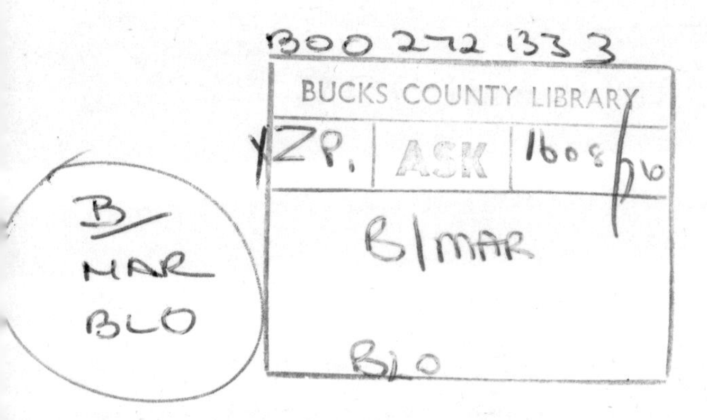

Filmset by
Specialised Offset Services Liverpool
Printed in Great Britain by
Lowe & Brydone Ltd

Contents

Illustrations

1

Girlhood

Queen Mary was born on 26th May 1867, in the same bedroom in which Queen Victoria had been born at Kensington Palace on 24th May 1819. For the little princess who was to receive a rather shattering string of names (Victoria Mary Augusta Louise Olga Pauline Claudine Agnes) it was an equally lovely day. The may smelt sweetly in Kensington Gardens, which stretched beyond the palace windows.

She was the first child of the young Prince Francis and Princess Mary Adelaide, Duke and Duchess of Teck, married but a brief time and very much in love. The Queen herself had offered them this suite, for at the time of the baby's coming they had no settled home. They had, of course, wanted a boy, an heir, but when she came both of them were grateful that she was a girl, with very fair hair and adorable blue eyes.

Queen Victoria came to see her, entering the room in which she herself had come into this world, as both nurses curtsied discreetly.

"To think that there is another little girl in *my* room," she said, and smiled, then, "I think she is rather like me."

The baby was indeed to prove this to be true, for both these queens were clever women when the hour came; both learnt the hard way.

Victoria had been born into a hard, cruel world, at a period of history when the extravagance of King George IV was a byword. Withering corpses hung from hillside gallows, both men and women were murdered nightly in the back alleys of London, and there the poor were poor indeed.

She had got her country out of the wretchedness it was in when she came to the throne, guided admirably by her good husband Albert, a man of great learning, much kindness, and tremendous forethought. He it was who made Victoria great.

The Queen was pleased with the new baby born in her own birth room forty-eight years later, where the nightingales sang at night, and one heard hardly any other sound but that of birds, or lambs bleating. Occasionally a farm cart rolled its way along the lane which today is Kensington High Street and there were cowslips in the vale. A very pleasant setting in which to be born.

Princess May's father and mother had met originally at a dinner party given in St James's Palace, and he had immediately been attracted to her prettiness, her utter charm, and her grace. It was said that he had been carried away utterly by her, and lost his heart to her then and there. He made a point of visiting her, and actually proposed marriage on only the second time that they met and went for a walk together in Kew Gardens, near Mary Adelaide's home. That was very much in accordance with the behaviour of the times, for this was the romantic era, when people fell in love at first sight. Queen Victoria had set the pattern, when two German brothers had come to visit her; the elder, England believed, was the future Prince Consort, the younger came to see England. But it had ended in the most charming romance which delighted the whole country, for Victoria (who, as Queen Regnant, had to do the proposing) fell for the younger brother, and Prince Ernest never forgave him.

Francis and Mary Adelaide were married with the usual ceremonial, and lived more or less happily ever after, save for financial troubles which for ever dogged their heels.

No decent family ever admitted this tiresome defect. It was vulgar to be 'hard-up'. But the Queen sympathized with them, and when she learnt that their first baby was on the way, she provided them with a roof over their heads – a process that was to be repeated as the Teck family grew.

At Kensington Palace it was comfortable, very pleasant, and

quiet. Of course, nobody thought Princess May would ever ascend the throne; she was just another little princess, cared for by a motherly old wet nurse, who sang her to sleep.

Life was peaceful and happy. After the birth of her first baby the Duchess of Teck stoutened quite enormously, and she never fined down again, which was a great worry to her.

"But I have the loveliest little baby in all the world," she said, and Princess May was certainly very pretty.

This was the period of the dinner party, starting in the late afternoon, and running well into the night or even early morning, and this certainly did not fine Mamma down.

But the family grew and living in Kensington Palace became too expensive for them. Their means were slender at a time when anybody who *was* anybody was rich, and creditors accumulated. It was hard to find somewhere cheaper, yet still suitable to their rank, especially when the outside world had to be persuaded that they had never known anything of financial trouble in their lives. To be poor was common!

After family discussions the Queen placed at their disposal a grace-and-favour mansion in Richmond Park. The White Lodge was cheaper, even if isolated and a little noisy in the rutting season when the stags made themselves heard. The little Princess had now three brothers, and they loved the change. It was a fairly quiet life, for the family could not afford extravagant entertainment, and Mary Adelaide believed in tranquillity for little children.

Occasionally the children of the Prince of Wales came to tea and played in the gardens. The young Princess liked the two boys, Albert Victor and George, and they helped her in the garden.

"They dig better than I do," she explained.

She was a determined little girl, interested in learning, though she never had the opportunities enjoyed by the Prince of Wales's children, for nobody bothered much about a daughter's lessons, on the principle that "she's bound to marry, anyway". An extravagant education could only be a waste of money!

The old Queen became attached to Princess May, and she said that "May has very nice manners", which was a great compliment, coming from her.

In reality her learning was sketchy. May saw little of the outside world, and it was not the best upbringing for a future queen, but it was all that her parents could afford for her. Possibly she was a little more boyish than most little girls of her era, for she had only her brothers to play with. Quite early in her career she must have been painfully aware that her people were hard-up, and their financial worries did not lessen with time.

In the end, it was quietly suggested that they go abroad for a time, where rents were lower and food cheaper, and they would not have to keep up the same style. They had heard that in Italy they would find living was cheaper, and it was not so vital to keep up appearances.

This period of their married life must have been harrowing for her parents but it happened to be all right for the little girl.

"Things are prettier here," she told her brothers, "and the people are so nice, and always so kind to us."

She was right in her first conclusion, for, during the second half of Queen Victoria's reign Great Britain was not renowned for beauty in furniture and housing, or for good taste. We went through a very bad phase at that period.

Reared in polite poverty, Princess May was well-mannered and obedient. She found the Italians most friendly, and she talked with them and mixed easily with them. She had a governess, of course, but the teaching of that time was not good. Her lessons might have been limited, but here she laid the cornerstone of her love of beautiful objects, china and glass, good furniture, and beautiful pictures. Being trained in Italy, she was far ahead of her times in experience of these things and her education in them.

I think she loved her time there; she certainly adored the Italians, who taught her so much, though, in the end, the family had to return to London for Princess May was growing up, which meant that they would now have to face the really large expense of her coming-out. It was the most inspiring moment of a girl's life, and the dream she had waited for all through her childhood. In the end they got suitable arrangements made for this great moment, even if her father said he would never be able to pay for it, and then what?

There was a private presentation at Court, for she was entitled to this from her relationship with the old Queen. She was received by Her Majesty in a drawing-room, where she made her curtsey.

Then there was her first ball when she was admitted more closely into the royal set.

She was never nervous, as the Prince of Wales's three shy daughters were, and she enjoyed every moment of it. She loved taking her place in the royal circle on the dais, and it was a tremendous thrill to know that she was grown up at last. Life spread a pathway thrillingly before her.

"But the expense!" said her father. "I can never meet it."

May long remembered the first 'deb' ball at which she wore the traditional snowy white of the society fledgling, her fair hair piled high, and everyone spoke of her may-blossom complexion. Then she had no scowl (that came in the thirties, and, of course, today could easily have been corrected, but not so at that time).

"I've come out!" she said bubbling with joy. "I'm grown up! Now everything that is wonderful begins!"

The old Queen was astute, but she was ageing quickly, and she wanted to get the dynastic future arranged whilst she still had the strength to do it. A bride was wanted for the eldest son of the Prince of Wales, Prince Albert Victor, Duke of Clarence, known to his close friends as Eddy and, as a result of one of his father's heavy jokes, as 'Prince Collar and Cuffs' because of his long neck and skinny arms! The Prince and Princess of Wales were good-looking, but this young man was somewhat weedy and sallow. Ultimately he would be King-Emperor. A bride had to be found for him.

Royal marriages were then arranged when those destined to play the leading roles were in their teens. They had no idea of what was being planned for them.

A pro-German lady, Queen Victoria had been deeply shocked by the way that her two elder daughters had been treated when they married Germans and went to live in Germany. She would not have admitted this, of course, but it *had* happened and she therefore had reservations about Germany. She therefore wanted Prince Eddy to marry an English girl, and she had her eye on Princess May!

The Princess Royal ("Pussy") had married the future Kaiser (both very much in love) and had been treated quite vilely by his father and mother in her adopted country, which infuriated the old Queen: they had never forgiven her for having a son with a withered arm. Queen Victoria was furious because she had sent an English gynaecologist over to be with her daughter, and he had never been permitted to go near her.

Her second daughter also had trouble.

For these reasons Queen Victoria drew the line at foreign marriages, and she looked to England for a wife for Eddy. At least he was gay and merry. The old Queen knew that she could trust May. She was well brought-up and conscientious, and this was what Victoria wanted in a future queen.

At that time every girl in London had her eye on Prince Albert Victor, he was *the* catch of the season, though I doubt if Princess May was likely to have her head turned.

She was a merry but cultured girl. Also, well aware of the gaps in her education, she was trying to build up her knowledge by wide reading.

She was enjoying every moment of her season (something of a frolic, so her brothers always said), and at this time she had little knowledge of what fate had in store for her.

It is true that her mother, who had the reputation of being the biggest chatterbox in society, might have dropped a hint or two, but Princess May would have felt it was wildly improbable.

Queen Victoria wanted to get the heir to the throne married to May before she died. At heart, she had never wished to go on living without her Albert, but she had a duty to the country to fulfil, and she had always carried out her duty faithfully and well.

She made the first move when she asked May to tea in the palace with one of her grand-daughters. It was a simple, rather homely little tea party.

"You liked your lessons?" she asked the girl.

Princess May confessed that she had never learnt sufficiently, and now, privately, she was reading more. The Queen admired this effort on her part. She also admitted that *she* had had a slack education, and had had to rely entirely on her adored late husband to guide her through the difficulties of the monarchy. And this he had done most nobly! She liked the young Princess's anxiety to improve herself. It was a strong point in her favour.

"And the season? You like the London season?" she asked.

Princess May confirmed that she adored every moment of it, though she knew that the financial strain was ageing her father, and they did not know how they would meet their debts. This she did *not* tell the Queen, it was too embarrassing! But she liked the Prince of Wales's children, though she knew little of Prince George, who was always away at sea. He was a born sailor, and had no ideas beyond it, so he always said.

The Wales children were on the whole fairly shy, save for the two boys (the youngest, Prince Alexander John Charles Albert, had died soon after birth). They lived mainly at Sandringham, which they loved, so they told Princess May. When they came to London they were usually very shy. On one occasion the three princesses, then in their teens, had come to tea at White Lodge, and on arrival stood about mutely, never asking anyone to sit down. Their hostess, an impatient woman, had said: "Aren't you ever going to ask us to sit down?"

Grandmamma objected to the fact that "they couldn't talk". "Princesses must learn to talk," said Victoria firmly, and she meant this. "Other people are naturally shy with them, and the duty of a prince or princess is to put them at their ease."

Princess May was very fond of Princess Maud, and during the season she met the princesses and Eddy at parties. She danced gaily, she was very pretty, and, having brothers, could talk to the men she met at an age when most debutantes were rather embarrassed.

"I can't think why," she told her mother. "On the whole I like boys better than girls, I think."

"You must *never* say that outside this place, or people will get wrong ideas about you," said Mamma.

Again the Queen asked the young girl down to visit her at Balmoral with her brother Adolphus ("Dolly"). It was a little worrying, for Victoria was never an easy woman to cope with. Growing older, she had not improved, and the loss of Albert was for ever in her mind, so that she was far more difficult to please. She could argue, but refused to be argued *with*! She expected the strictest obedience from visitors, and humility to an exceptional degree. It did not make life easy!

She asked May all sorts of questions, for she was determined that the marriage of the heir to the throne should be to the girl on whom she personally could rely, and whom she knew would do the right thing.

On the morning of her return home Princess May said to her mother: "I'm very thankful that is over! It is very difficult, for half the time she doesn't hear, and when she *does* hear she doesn't seem to like it!"

In her diary the old Queen wrote:

> May is a particularly nice girl, so quiet, so cheerful, and very carefully brought up. She has grown very pretty.

Now that was a great compliment, for Victoria never hesitated to notice something that she did *not* like in people, and would put her reactions into English vehemently.

The girl was fairly tall, in a period when women were not tall, but she never showed any sign of her mother's most unfortunate stoutness (which had been a tragedy to the Duchess of Teck).

For her daughter's coming-out, the Duchess had taken a furnished house in Grosvenor Place. Her parents could not afford it, but would have done anything for darling May. Unfortunately the money just disappeared.

May had grown up from something of a tree-climbing tomboy with her brothers into a merry girl who was fond of fun.

The Prince of Wales heartily agreed with his mother's choice; he liked Princess May, and thought that an English-bred bride would be a very good idea for this country. There had been sufficient trouble with his elder sister marrying the future German Emperor, and then having that nasty little son of hers, said he. (At that time, of course, he never knew how *very* nasty that son would be!)

"An English girl for England, yes, that might be a very good plan," said Queen Victoria.

She thought that darling May was a sweet girl, and had been very impressed that she was doing private reading, because she thought that her education had not been good enough.

"In her own way, she's clever," said the old lady.

Eddy and May saw a lot of one another during that first season, and already the Press had an eye on them, for there were references in the paper preparing the public for the announcement of the coming marriage.

The girl had no idea of it! She was dancing through this first season, and making the most of it. On 3rd December 1891, the Prince of Wales wrote to his mamma from Marlborough House.

> You may, I think, make your mind quite easy about Eddy, and that he has made up his mind to propose to May. She is coming to us after Christmas, and then we are sure that all will be settled.

Without doubt, the girl herself knew nothing of what was going on, for, at that time, mothers did not confide in their daughters. Mamma would never have breathed a word of it, but she must have been radiant with joy! All the world knew that the Queen thought that May was a darling, and a dear girl! She liked her! But the Princess was not for the moment interested in marriage, and when the news came it was one of the big surprises of her life.

Her first season had been great fun; she loved seeing the dawn break while she was still dancing! She was popular and pretty, a radiant personality, who brought the right touch to any party. But of course her parents were distressed about their only daughter's season, and the way that the bills were mounting up.

"I can't see how we shall ever pay for it," said her mother.

Meanwhile Princess May was still catching up on her education. She visited churches and museums all over London, broadening her knowledge. She was horrified by the poverty that she saw in the East End; people and especially children walking around barefoot, even in the snow.

"It is so shocking to see that," she said. "Surely something could be done to help them?"

Now the newspapers, so far content with speculation, began to take a renewed interest in her, as if they knew something. She danced often with Prince Eddy. At first the papers had written of the Prince as a probability, then it seemed that he was more than that. He would have to marry soon, and the young Princess was pretty, gay, most amusing, and the right person. She could dance all night and never wilt! Surely she was the suitable bride for the heir to the throne?

May had already had three proposals, and had turned them all down. She was too young, she said and, for the present, life was too gaily amusing for her to want to be anything but a deb!

Time moved on. There was Cowes Week, and a visit to the Queen again, rather a dull one, for if anybody could be insistent and demanding it was that old lady! The Princess was well aware of the public interest in herself, but not of their speculations, and for the moment went on gaily.

Towards the end of 1891 the newspapers began a whispering

campaign. Whom would Prince Eddy marry? When would it be? Surely it was about time for the wedding bells to ring for a future king?

The Princess received an invitation to a pre-Christmas party which was going to be held in the old-fashioned manner, at Luton Hoo, country home of the Danish Minister, and all Society was due to be there (save those going down to Sandringham for the great occasion). This was to be a very special party, with dancing and Christmas trees, carol singers, and all the right background.

Princess Mary accepted an invitation with joy. One was only young once, and she was making the most of it. Prince Albert Victor would be there to give a cachet to the affair, and it should be exciting. It meant some new dresses (which worried her father), but this had to be arranged. As her mother said, "We have only the one daughter, and we must do everything that we possibly can to help her. We'll find the money somehow."

May went off in triumph. On the first night there was a wonderful dinner, and then dancing. She whirled around the floor with Prince Eddy.

He said, "Let's go into the sitting-out room, because there is something that I want to talk to you about."

They went into the conservatory, beautifully decorated and with subdued lighting; she always remembered how sweetly it smelt of flowers, which she adored. He put an arm around her (which perhaps, as a young man of the world, was not unusual for him) and then asked her to marry him.

"You know what the papers are saying?" he said. "And *I* think it is a good idea!"

It was one of the supreme moments of her life. So young, just out, with a wonder year behind her, and now the future King of England asking her to be his queen! She had a very deep affection for him; she was not the sort of girl to fall passionately in love, but she was the type which loves dearly and for ever.

She liked the thought of their spending their lives together, each being a help to the other. I do not suppose that the idea of being Queen occurred to her for the time being, but she *had* a fondness for him, and this would have ripened into a lasting love, she thought.

That night she found the time to write in her diary that Eddy had asked her to marry him, and she had said "Yes". She commented on how very happy both of them were.

There had never been a time in their lives when they had not known each other, and s ıı saw ahead of her the happiest of lives. She was not the girl to shirk responsibility (everyone knew this) and being a queen would perhaps mean that she did not get as much of the home life that she loved.

"Oh, well, that's a long way off!" said he, cheerfully.

Royal engagements never last for very long, and before Princess May knew where she was, she was off to see her future grandmother-in-law again.

"Such a sweet, *dear* girl!" was what the old Queen said, and she added: "I am sure that she will make an *excellent* Queen Consort."

Plans went forward speedily, almost too quickly for the bride-to-be, for she was nearly whirled off her feet. It was arranged that they would live in St James's Palace, which pleased her very much because she had always loved the antiquity of this palace, and its royal associations.

"I love old places," she said. History fascinated her. She admired old furniture, china, and glass, and read books about them, but the Prince thought that "a bit of a waste of time", and she laughed at the idea.

"I shall *always* love old things," she said.

She was privately a wee bit annoyed that he had earned himself the name of Prince Collar-and-Cuffs (much to the fury of the old Queen, who thought that it was practically *lèse-majesté*). But there was nothing that she could do about it. He had a very long neck, and very long arms. He had inherited his father's charming gaiety of manner, and was full of the joys of living, whereas his brother, Prince George (dedicated to the Royal Navy) was far more solemn.

For the Tecks the thrill of May's engagement to the Queen's future successor was tempered by reflections of the cost of the wedding. They were almost on the rocks! In the end the Royal Family came to their aid and helped them out as the preparations went forward early in 1892.

In those days a trousseau, even for a quite humble person, meant twelve of everything in the lingerie line, and a future Queen-Empress would need three times that. She must have the right dresses for her new position as Duchess of Clarence, and shoddy stuff would not do for her! Her parents must have contemplated the marriage with cold horror.

She said reluctantly, "I'm not so fond of clothes, really, quite happy in any old thing, but this *is* rather different."

I think it was the Prince of Wales who helped her people out, for he was always a very generous man, and most kind.

Whatever happened, the girl must have the suitable clothes for her new position, and no wonder the thought horrified her hard-up parents, already in debt for her 'season'! I do not imagine that the old Queen did too much, for she had always been economy-minded, but she *did* promise to cover the costs of the reception, and the expenses of the ceremony itself.

The date for the marriage was finally given out as being 27th February, which did not give them a lot of time to get this tremendous trousseau made, and the marriage planned. The country would expect a right royal ceremony for them.

The Queen disapproved of long engagements, and she was the one who finally fixed the date. Her eldest son was enchanted about it all, and he tried to persuade his mother to appear at the marriage, abandoning her deep mourning and coming forth gloriously as the Queen of England, for this *was* a very special occasion.

Not she!

He told her that this would give her people a very real thrill (and it would have done) but she was absolutely resolute, and nothing in this world would get her out of crêpe and the deepest black. She preferred her widow's cap to the crown, so she said.

"But the people want this of you," he begged. "It would help the country."

She summed it up in five words: "It would not help *me*" was what she said.

You could not do very much with her, when she got determined, as he often found. In the end she broke down and said that, when she had lost her husband, she had lost her entire world, and only prayed to die. He did beg her to remember the demands of the country, and respect their wishes, but she was not that sort of woman. She would wear deep mourning for Albert until the day that she died, and she stuck to that.

Now, of course, the Princess was fêted wherever she went, and she had an invitation to go down to Sandringham for Christmas and spend it there with the Prince and Princess of Wales and their family. She had always been deeply attracted by this favourite home of the Prince of Wales. She said to a friend, "Sandringham is such a *happy* place," which was the way that they all found it. (And *extraordinarily*, so much that is *unhappy* has happened to them there, yet they still love it.)

They went down by train. May found that her fiancé had a bad cold, which he simply could not shake off. It had been rather a difficult autumn for the Prince and Princess. Among other things, their second son George had been most critically ill with typhoid fever. He had always enjoyed very good health, so they had hardly expected this, and there had been a couple of days when they thought that he could not live. He recovered only because he was a very strong young man, and now had gone back to sea. The Princess of Wales was now concerned for her elder son; he had caught cold out on some dreadful parade, where he had had to be, and the day was deadly chilly.

"He must be nursed, and we can do that at Sandringham," she said.

On Christmas Eve, Princess May wrote in her diary:

> Goodbye to 1891, a most eventful year. Eddy is still ill with this bad cold, and his sister is ill, too.

Little did she know, as she hailed the New Year, that the most terrible ordeal lay ahead for her. She loved Sandringham, adoring the park, and the very rural look. "It must be heaven in rhododendron time," she said.

Early in the New Year a 'pea-souper' fog settled down on them, blotting out everything. It affected the whole of England, and lasted some days. Prince Eddy was still nursing this wretched cold and, sick of being indoors, spoke of it as "this imprisonment". When the fog lifted he said that, even if it made him worse, he was going out with the guns for he was sick to death of being kept indoors.

He did go out, but he came back fairly quickly, for he felt so much worse that he could do nothing else. It was then that the family – preparing special celebrations for Eddy's twenty-eighth birthday – thought that there must be something really wrong with him, and although he did try to come down to open his birthday presents, on the morning of 28th January he found that he simply could not do it! Princess May was now really worried.

"I am sure it is more than a bad cold," she kept saying. "People get over *colds* fairly quickly."

Soon the whole world knew that the ultimate heir to the throne was very seriously ill at Sandringham, the latest victim of an influenza epidemic that was sweeping much of Europe.

Princess May was distracted on the day that our greatest specialist came down from London, to be met at the railway station and brought to the house. Everyone had great confidence in him, but, of course, he had been called much too late, and the virus had already undermined Eddy's frail constitution.

"But, surely, there is something that can be done ... something to help him?" Princess May gasped when her future father-in-law told her of the diagnosis, and the dreadful news that there was no hope for him!

The family clustered around his bed knowing that the end was coming. Princess Mary stood just behind the Princess of Wales, who sat by the bed, her dying son in her arms.

It must have been quite shocking for this poor young girl, but she had infinite courage. As the Prince lay there he whispered to his mother, "Someone is calling me."

A highly devout woman, and very religious, she said, "It is Jesus who is calling you, Eddy," and she held him in her arms until he died.

To the poor young girl standing just behind her (and who had never gazed upon death before) cold horror came! It was the greatest shock of her life so far. They helped her away, and the Prince of Wales did what he could to comfort her, but there are times when that is not possible. They were to have been married in a few weeks' time, and the gay thrill of a royal marriage had now turned to the bleak horror of a funeral. Very few people would have realized how she felt, for, although they had only been engaged for a short time, they had known one another since toddling days, and she could not imagine a world without him.

England was plunged into the deepest mourning, and the old Queen was perhaps more shattered than anyone else, but she did think affectionately of the poor girl who was to have been her new grand-daughter-in-law.

She wrote to a friend, saying, "May is like a crushed flower," which was only too true.

Nobody had even thought of the possibility of such a terrible thing, but probably the one man most dismayed was poor Prince George, Eddy's brother, who had dedicated his whole life to the Royal Navy, which he adored, and now, as heir to the throne, he would have to abandon it. He would have to live at Court and give his life to his country, training to wear the crown that he had never wanted.

Princess May wrote sympathetically to him, for she knew him well, and grieved for him. Both were sharing a sorrow much deeper than anything they had known before. She said, "It is all too dreadful, one goes on because one *has* to do so, but it is too pathetic!"

When the funeral was over, the girl returned to White Lodge, into the arms of Mamma. Now, in the attics, her enormous trousseau was stored, and what to do with it nobody knew.

It was a very cold spring. Even the Thames was frozen over, and people walked across it. The Prince and Princess of Wales were very good to the girl who should have been their daughter-in-law and I believe that the Prince helped with some of the financial troubles which were now quite bewildering for the poor Tecks. But the person most upset was Prince George, and the girl knew that he needed sympathy perhaps more than she did. His entire career had been wrecked utterly, as he said. He had always told her, "Eddy can keep the crown, it's not my idea! I want a ship, a crown would *not* be my idea at all."

And now it would come to him!

Princess May had enjoyed a very contented childhood, and she found it difficult to believe that such a terrible thing could have happened to her. She lost weight, and went very pale. The doctors advised a change of scene for her (there were too many memories of her dead fiancé at home), and she ought to be taken abroad for a short while. Somehow the Tecks found the money for this, and her mother took her to Cannes on the French Riviera. There she was frequently visited by Prince George. Afterwards her parents took her to Germany. She had always been a very sensible girl, who knew there was no point in looking back, and during her time abroad she flung herself into her old hobby of seeing lovely churches, of visiting curio shops, and learning about rare pictures, beautiful furniture, and exquisite china and glass. She had the chance to do this, and the antique dealers recognized and respected her enthusiasm and taught her a lot that she wanted to learn. All her life she said that she had every reason to be deeply grateful to them – especially those whom she had met on her earlier visit to Italy.

She wrote to a friend: "These men taught me everything that I know, and they were quite wonderful to me. I think they saved me, and gave me something else to think about."

When she returned to England she went to a party or two, and she felt that the loneliness of the countryside helped her. She would never forget how she had met death for the first time, and the horror of it still stayed.

She did not want to meet people, and she said so.

Her mother was a help, a very wise woman who let her do exactly what she liked best, and at this hour in her life she turned again to the hobbies of her teens. She was heart-broken. It was some time before they heard that gay laughter of hers again. Then her mother wrote to her father:

> May has laughed again, and what a joy that is!

When she returned to White Lodge, Prince George was one of her first visitors. They had a sorrow to share, both of them had suffered a bad loss, he more than she, for he had had to give up the Royal Navy.

They went down to Sandringham to stay with the family. There the bedroom in which Eddy had died was kept as if he were still in this world. Queen Victoria had started this fashion when the Prince Consort died and it was kept up by the Princess of Wales. There were flowers in the room, and the bed was covered by a satin Union Jack, whilst soap was on the washstand, and Eddy's hair brushes on the dressing-table.

Prince George and Princess May together visited Eddy's tomb at Windsor. Gradually Princess May found herself drawn to Prince George: they understood each other and she sympathized when he said that having been forced to leave the Navy, he now had to "work for my living", as he put it. They talked together, he about his shattered career and how everything had changed, she about her deep sorrow. A new spring was born, and they comforted one another, a comfort that she did not get from others. That brief engagement of hers, with marriage only a few weeks ahead, was now a dead dream, of course, and when she spoke of her unused trousseau in the attic she said: "It will never be wanted now."

The two saw of lot of each other and companionship blossomed into love. May and Prince George – previously created Duke of York – became engaged on 3rd May 1893. Possibly they were not at that time deeply in love, but sympathy is a strong tie, and they had always been fond of one another. The announcement of the engagement enchanted England, for the country had felt deep sympathy for both of them. The *Morning Post* wrote:

> On this account alone the felicitations offered to the Duke of York will be both spontaneous and sincere.

The paper summed up the general view that George had pleased himself and delighted the nation by his choice of a bride.

The country was overwhelmed at the prospect of the marriage in July. They thought of him as 'The Sailor Prince' and of her as 'The Daughter of England'.

On the day that the engagement was announced, the Duke dined at White Lodge where he found his future mother-in-law something of a chatterbox. He said to a friend, "*How* that woman talks!" The Queen was enchanted, for she had always felt that dear May would make a charming consort, and she was right. "May is an old-fashioned girl," the Queen said.

England believed that the second brother was nearer the young girl's heart than the elder one had been. He was the more attractive man, but obstinate as a mule, a man who would stand no nonsense. May wrote to him:

> I would very much like to give you a wedding ring, if you will wear it for my sake. I herewith send you one or two to try for size. Let me have the one you choose at once, and I will give it you in the chapel ... I love you with all my heart.
>
> May

And to her old governess she wrote:

> Georgie is a dear ... He adores me ...

But the bridegroom did not understand her devotion to antiques, china and glass. They had, in fact, few subjects in common.

Once more England worked up into a thrill, capping it with: "Oh, I do hope nothing dreadful happens this time." There need be no delay, for everyone knew that a complete trousseau was lying at White Lodge all ready for the day.

Mary of Teck, aged 5, with her mother and brothers

Princess May with her parents

2

Marriage and Children

Good weather was forecast and it came, which was the first joy of that morning. Some people spent most of the night waiting in the streets, and at dawn enormous crowds arrived to be sure of getting a good place from which to see the procession. All the world wished them well, for they had had more than their fair share of misfortune. It was *the* wedding of the year.

The bride slept late, and woke radiant. She wore the white satin dress which is the rule for brides, most exquisitely embroidered, and with it a very small wedding veil. This was commented on (rather disapprovingly by some), but the veil was pinned with a most glorious diamond White Rose of York to her fair hair, which looked intensely lovely.

Two future queens followed her to her marriage (both children at the time). One was Princess Margaret of Connaught, who when the time came would go to the throne of Sweden as its queen; the other, the younger, fair-headed little Princess Ena of Battenberg, who would marry King Alfonso XIII of Spain. (He was the only crowned head in Europe who was born a king, and it was said that the midwife curtseyed to him when he was born!)

The wedding dress itself was utterly magnificent, and how her parents managed to afford it is a mystery, for they were always having financial problems and I should have thought this royal marriage was undoubtedly their heaviest one! Perhaps the old Queen (who was a very rich old lady) stretched out a helping hand to provide for the enormous demands which this sort of wedding must make on the family purse. Most certainly the kind

Prince of Wales, again, would have been generous.

Later in the day the Duke and Duchess left for Sandringham, the home of the Royal Family where they could live, as she put it, "like ordinary people, and how nice!"

They were welcomed by the entire village, which was garlanded; the villagers had put up quite a magnificent show. All the world and its wife was there to welcome them. They went straight to York Cottage, which for many years to come was going to be their favourite home. It was a wedding gift from the Prince of Wales. At the moment it was small, and used mainly as a sort of 'spare part' for the big house itself. Bachelor guests used to sleep there when the big house was overflowing. But the Duke and Duchess fell in love with the place, even if it was cramped at times. It was most lovely when the rhododendrons were out and from the windows they could see rose bushes and, between them, glimpses of the lake where, in winter, they skated.

York Cottage was small, you could almost have called it poky, for the Prince of Wales, who gloried in his holidays at the big Sandringham House itself, had not bothered too much with the cottage. It was smugly Victorian, not pretty, and, for a girl deeply interested in good furniture, this must have been worrying. But the Prince of Wales had given it to them for their own, and for the first time in her life May would not have to worry over the financial side of the business. She made plans for changing the cottage. It was her first chance to show her genius for design. The Duke was not inspired by her ideas; like a lot of men he had some difficulty in seeing what she meant by her own improvements.

She was devoted to her father-in-law, who was kindness itself and would do anything for them, but her mother-in-law Alexandra worried her, for May could never tell if the Princess of Wales had heard what she said, Alexandra would never admit to being deaf, which of course complicated everything and very frequently she went off with quite the wrong ideas about what had been said. But no-one could have been kinder than the stoutening Prince of Wales, always so understanding and tolerant.

Years later, actually a short while after she had become Queen, she wrote of this time and she stated;

> I sometimes think that, after we were married, we were not left alone enough. Somehow we had not the opportunity to understand one another as quickly as we might have otherwise done.

The royal life is for ever disturbed by messengers, by missions, by work to be done, and visitors to be seen. In May's case, of course, she was rarely free from surprise visits from her mother-in-law and her sisters-in-law. She had come from a very happy-go-lucky home where she could do what she wished, for her parents were 'spoilers', she always said. She laughed a lot, she was used to playing with her brothers, was good at cricket (which surprised the Duke of York), and was far more gay at heart than her photographs suggested. She photographed badly. That worried her mother, for, as she said, people do not know how pretty May is, and what a lovely smile she has!

She found her husband difficult at times, because he instantly resented it if one did not conform immediately to his wishes.

She did not argue, but concurred in what he said, hoping in time to persuade him to change commands into something gentler.

She made extensive changes at York Cottage and was very clever about it. When she first mentioned her plans to him he doubted her judgement. But when she said that she had arranged to fit in a billiards room (he was very keen on billiards) he fell in with her ideas immediately!

"I love houses," she said. "There is so much one can do to a house if only one tries hard enough."

That autumn one of the Teck aunts died, which sent the Court into mourning, led of course by Queen Victoria, who seized any chance to plunge them all into black. Then there was half-mourning for the usual time. Later May did manage to go to Cowes for the Week. She went over to see the old Queen, who greeted her with the utmost affection, and wrote about it in her diary, saying what a dear child she was. "I can't tell you how pleased we all are with May ..."

She was, of course, far more attractive than contemporary studies of her indicated for she had such beautiful colouring, and very clear blue eyes, and she could smile radiantly. She was amusing to talk to, and she laughed a lot. Her photographs never seemed to show her spiritual qualities.

She found it amazing not to be short of money (though this would never make her extravagant, for she was not that sort of personality). She made friends with people around Sandringham, and they were surprised at her amiability, and the fact that, although she could be dignified (and was) she never put on grand airs.

York Cottage emerged from its intensive alterations. She had made quite a new place of it. She herself was surprised by the changes she had wrought, rising and falling on her toes as she described them – something that she always did when she was excited (even into old age). She did it in Westminster Abbey when she first found herself planning what a lovely background it would be for the marriage of her daughter, and she said with delight in her voice, "We must *always* have the Abbey for royal weddings. Then everybody can see it, and it is such a glorious background."

Soon it was announced that she was *enceinte*.

It was decided that her first baby (expected in the June following her wedding) should be born at her mother's house, White Lodge in Richmond Park, where she had been brought up. Her mother was thrilled, and the prospect of a new heir to the throne was the talk of that hot summer of 1894.

"I do hope that it is going to be a boy," his mother said.

"If he isn't, you'll have a son next time," her father said. "I shouldn't worry too much. Boys run in our family."

The baby arrived on 23rd June, the very day of Richmond Fair, when all the world and its wife were in the streets of the little town, with hurdy-gurdys going, galloping horses, swing boats, and everybody there. Previously to this it had seemed that the Queen was getting a little worried, and she had written:

> May keeps us waiting a little, but it must be soon now ...

And again, in her private diary, a day or two later, as her impatience grew: "No telegram from dear May."

But early on the day of the fair the rumour went around that the doctors had gone to White Lodge, and later a marquee was put up on the lawn, and in it was the visitors' book in which those who wished to inquire after the royal baby and his mother could sign their names.

It is always said (I heard it first as a child and believe it is no trumped-up story) that a gipsy fortune-teller when she was told that a future King of England had been born shook her head and said: "He may be the future King of England, but he will never be the *crowned* King." Most unfortunately that gipsy's warning was borne out.

The Queen next day took a train from Windsor for Richmond, which was something of an effort, and there she drove through the remains of the fairground to the park and on to White Lodge to see the sturdy little boy, her first great-grandson. He was fair like his mother, and quite a big boy, which the nurses said was why he had been late in arriving. That night the old Queen wrote in her diary:

> It seems that it has never happened in this country that there be three direct heirs as well as the Sovereign alive.

From the first time that she had been told of May's pregnancy she had predicted that her first-born would be a son, because "dear May always did the right thing". When the old lady saw him he was lying in the royal cradle, which had been made for the Princess Royal and had been brought from Buckingham

Palace to receive him, as it had received his father and his grandfather before him.

He was a month old when he was baptized in the silver-gilt font, also brought from Windsor Castle for this great occasion. He was the first baby of the new generation to wear the royal christening robe, which is made of Honiton lace and was originally designed for the Princess Royal. After that, each of the old Queen's children wore it in turn.

There was some difficulty over his names, but the Queen was very good at choosing this sort of thing and she prevailed. The baby was named Edward Albert Christian George Andrew Patrick David, the last four names being those of the patron saints of England, Scotland, Ireland and Wales; but in the family he was always known as David. When he went to Osborne as a Royal Navy cadet (as his father wished) he was known as 'Sardine', being the opposite of whales!

When the Princess recovered she went that August on holiday to St Moritz which the Prince of Wales vowed was the best place in the world to get really strong again. The Duke of York would have gone with her and her mother, but at the last moment he cried off. The truth was that he had been worried by the eternal chattering of his mother-in-law and simply could not face up to another hour of it! To a friend, he wrote:

> I am very fond of Maria, but I could not go through the six weeks that I spent there again ...

Maybe his wife realized that this was not unwarranted, for Mamma had always been a chatterbox, so she went alone with Mamma on this holiday, travelling incognito as 'Lady Killarney'. She could quite understand that the eternal talk got on her husband's nerves. "He wasn't brought up to it, like I was," she once commented.

She returned to York Cottage and was very glad to get there. It was in the October that bad news came – the unexpected death of the Czar of Russia. Alexander III had been ill for some time, and was only forty-nine years of age, married to Dagmar, a Danish princess, sister of the Princess of Wales. His death again plunged the Court at Windsor into deep mourning.

"I shall never like mourning." the Duchess of York said, "it only stresses the sadness, and is, I am sure, all wrong." But Queen Victoria was very insistent about it and it was, of course, highly fashionable. It was a most unfortunate thing that this death came just at the moment when the marriage of the Czarevitch Nicholas to the Princess Alice of Hesse ('Alicky') had been planned. She was the granddaughter of the old Queen, and had refused to marry Prince Eddy when it was suggested to her. It was said that she and the new Czar were very much in love.

In the late November the Czar was buried, with a service that lasted for two and a half hours. The Duke of York was one of the pall bearers, and got very tired of the whole affair. "They'll never get me over here to another of these funerals. They last too long!" he said.

He and the Czar Nicholas II were almost doubles. The likeness was amazing. But the Duke of York was very worried about the extreme poverty and hunger in Russia; there must be ghastly unhappiness, he said, in contrast to the splendour and vivid extravagance of the Court life where not a rouble was spared.

Ultimately it transpired that, although the whole Court was in deep mourning, the new Czar did not intend to set aside the original plans for his coming marriage to Prince Alice of Hesse, and 'Nicky' and 'Alicky' were married almost immediately in the chapel of the Winter Palace. No good will come of this, the people predicted, and the whole affair seemed to be under a cloud, the seers predicting that they would pay for it in blood and fire, which unfortunately came only too true not many years later! The Duke of York was upset to be away from his wife so long, and he wrote to her:

> I really believe that I should get ill if I had to be away from you for a long time.

He and his pretty wife were devoted to each other now. They had married when both of them were saddened, she by the death of his elder brother, he by the fact that he would have to abandon the career in the Royal Navy, to qualify as heir to the throne and, as he put it, "learn the job I *don't* want!"

Their second child was born on 20th December of the following year at York Cottage, where he had not been expected until the late January. It was very cold weather and the lake was frozen. The Yorks were having a skating party when Prince Albert suddenly made it understood that he was on his way! This caused a panic at York Cottage, for it was a matter of major importance to get the Home Secretary down to Sandringham from London. He always had to be in attendance at a royal birth, since the time of James II had come under suspicion of having had a baby boy smuggled into his wife's bedchamber to ensure the succession in the male line.

My father (we are all Norfolk people) told me that when the train with the Home Secretary in it steamed into Wolferton station, the visitor literally dived into the waiting carriage, and the horses galloped to York Cottage only just in time. It was a race between them and the coming babe. I have always wondered what would have happened if they had not reached York Cottage in time, and the baby *had* arrived. Would it have made any difference to his future crown? Fortunately that constitutional problem did not arise.

Today this ungracious duty has ceased to be, for it ended when that very baby – named after his great-grandfather the Prince Consort – grew up and inherited a crown which one is sure he did not want! It ended when his second daughter Princess Margaret Rose was born at Glamis Castle, the home of her grandparents. The Home Secretary (Mr John Clynes) had been away on his summer holiday and was called back and delayed quite a time, for the little girl came late – "And this," said George VI-to-be, "is the *last* time this happens!"

There was another complication. The baptism of the baby at the royal font, with water from the River Jordan, was deferred because Prince Henry of Battenberg died quite unexpectedly.

It was the era of royal mourning in a big way, and once again the Court was plunged into the deepest black. The Duchess of Teck's sister, the Grand Duchess Augusta of Mecklenburg-Strelitz, said, rather aptly, that "she could not see why a baby could not be made a Christian because poor Henry had died!"

The Yorks were very happy at Sandringham, where they lived the life of a country gentleman and his wife. The Duchess adored it. In the year of the Diamond Jubilee – on 26th April 1897 – their third child was born, the little girl whom they both wanted so much. "After all," her mother said, "my son's my son till he gets him a wife, but my daughter's my daughter all her life!" She little knew how true that would be for the princess then. Quite a lot of well-wishers wrote to the Duke of York suggesting that the new baby be called Diamond. This also was the Queen's wish, but the Prince of Wales objected that it would always give away her age, so she was baptized Victoria Alexandra Alice Mary, was known as the Princess Victoria during the old Queen's remaining days, then as Princess Mary. Her birth enchanted the Duke and Duchess, and also Mrs Bill, their nurse.

The Diamond Jubilee was a tremendous affair arranged with a commemoration service on the steps of St Paul's Cathedral, *not* inside it as originally intended, for it was found that the poor old lady could not walk that far. She had grown very infirm indeed.

London was quite shocked when they realized how old she had become, and how difficult it was for her to follow the service, for she had to be helped all the time. She was, of course, as courageous as ever, but she needed a great deal of assistance.

"She is very brave to do it," said the Duchess of York.

The bells rang out all day, and magnificent china mugs were presented to every child in the land, with a picture of the Queen on them and the label *Longest and most glorious reign*.

This was the most wonderful day in the whole of English history, so the newspapers said.

While preparations for the Diamond Jubilee were going

forward the Yorks were hurriedly summoned to White Lodge, where the Duchess of Teck had been taken ill. She was still enormously stout (she had never managed to conquer this affliction) and during the spring she had undergone a rather nasty operation. It had not been entirely satisfactory, though she was up and about again, but not well. Although in pain, she took part in the Jubilee procession.

Suddenly a second operation was needed, and her daughter rushed to her. It all took place in White Lodge, where they had to break the news to the Duchess of York that Mary Adelaide had died under the anaesthetic. She could not believe that life could ever be quite the same again, for the bond between her and her mother had been so close.

The Duchess of Teck, one of the last of the Hanoverians, was buried in the vaults at Windsor (a place which everyone detested, for nothing could have been more horrible, but this was where they lay). At the time, May felt that she would never recover from the shock of her mother's death, for they had been so devoted. Also her father had aged considerably, and the loss of his wife put still more years on to him. His brain had begun to fail, and there were moments when he was not sure of what he was doing, or even of what he was saying.

They made arrangements for him to live on under male nurses at White Lodge, because it was the background to which he was accustomed, and he was too old to break away. A doctor saw him daily, but he went downhill.

He died in the January of the new century, and by that time he could not even recognize his own children. It was a merciful release. He died unaware that he had lived into the 'terrible' twentieth century, at least.

3

Princess of Wales

It was not until the January of 1901 that, quite suddenly, the Queen began to fail. She had gone out for her morning ride in the gardens of Osborne in a bath-chair, as usual, but when the time for the afternoon ride came she said that she was too tired. She took to her bed, never to rise again.

The new King Edward VII and his nephew Kaiser Wilhelm II of Germany (always her favourite grandchild) wrapped her in her wedding veil, and together they lifted her into her coffin. Edward had always detested the Kaiser, and vowed that he would never trust him an inch but, whatever anyone else said, he *had* been the old lady's pet.

Princess May now became Princess of Wales, and she was very deeply affected. She had always been very appreciative of the old Queen's integrity, though, like everyone else, was afraid of her, for she could change so suddenly! It had been difficult taking her great-grandchildren to see her, in horror that one of them would do something dreadful, for "Gangan" would never excuse a fault. She wrote:

> I cannot tell you how affected I am at the poor Queen's death, as she was always so kind to me, and ever a good friend and counsellor.

This, of course, was not entirely true, for the old lady could be dictatorial and commanding. She *would* have her own way, and on one occasion the poor princess had come out of the old Queen's room, almost collapsing, and said, in her anxiety, "I simply can't stand another moment of this."

In 1901, when the end was near, May and George hurried to

Osborne. In her diary on 22nd January the Duchess of York wrote:

> We got to Osborne at 5.30, only just in time to see beloved Grandmamma alive, for she passed away at 6.30, surrounded by all of us.

On 27th January she wrote a long letter to her Aunt Augusta in Germany, telling her about it:

> Now she lies in her coffin in the drawing room, which is beautifully arranged as a chapel. The coffin is covered with the coronation robes; and her little diamond crown, and the garter, lie on a cushion above her head. Guardsmen watch her day and night, and it is so impressive and fine, you would admire it, if you could see it all.

It was, of course, an interminable funeral coming across the water from the Isle of Wight to the mainland, and the crown of England blazing in the January sunlight, a most wonderful sight! Most of the kings in Europe (and we had many at that time) followed her.

But for the new Princess of Wales there was a note of sadness, for this was going to be the end of their country life at Sandringham, which she adored, and they would have to live in Marlborough House, a larger home, of course, but they would lose the large garden that she loved for her children to play in. They would *have* to live there. She redecorated and arranged the house, a work which interested her. The 'big house' would be their country home, and Marlborough House their London seat. "For the moment it is perplexing," she wrote to a friend, "but we shall find ourselves, given time."

Her alterations to Marlborough House were extensive, for she and Queen Alexandra, the previous tenant, had totally different ideas. She made structural changes, got rid of all those ornaments, and simplified the layout for the servants. In the planning process they had walked miles, she said.

Osborne House was not empty. The new monarch turned it into a training college for cadets for the Royal Navy, which everyone knew Queen Victoria would have liked.

The new occupants of Marlborough House, however much they had changed the interior, just could not make the garden bigger, or less public, for the children to play in. Crowds would collect to watch them playing.

"It is so *bad* for them," said the Princess of Wales. "We all ought to have *some* private life." But she had to be given time.

Becoming the Princess of Wales was not easy, of course: one had to stay calm, was the way that she put it. Mrs Bill was the big help she always had been. I knew Mrs Bill in her retirement living in a grace-and-favour house near Sandringham; my husband used to mow her lawn for her, whilst we talked.

She was then in her eighties, and all through the summer she would bicycle down to the beach to bathe! She adored Princess May.

"Oh, she was so wonderful, and she did have such a lot of trouble, too," she told me. "It was a shame. Haven't you noticed in life, it is always the nice people who get the trouble?"

Mrs Bill had become far more than Nannie to the household of the Princess of Wales, who relied on her. When she and her husband went off on that terribly long tour abroad – to Australia, New Zealand, Canada and South Africa – Mrs Bill fixed up a map on the nursery wall, an enormous one, and first thing every day she took the children to see "where Daddy and Mummy were at this moment". Their places of call were then marked by a pin with a small flag on it. Naturally Mrs Bill disapproved of long absences from the family, but what could you do when the parents were the future King and Queen?

"It isn't right at all," said Mrs Bill, "but it was part of their work, and they had to do it, and so we sort of got used to it."

Queen Alexandra had been fifty-six when she came to the throne for which she had waited such a long time, but she carried her years most beautifully. Unfortunately she had this wretched deafness, which increased (though she would not admit it), nor would she ever agree that she had not heard a single word that was said! This made it very difficult to talk to her.

Both she and the King were devoted to their grandchildren, but the trouble was that they spoilt them abominably. This spoiling was a great worry to Mrs Bill, who loathed the thought of sweets in bed (*after* the teeth had been brushed) and insisted that, even if you were the King of England, nursery rules should *not* be broken.

When their parents were away on these long tours, whenever they could the King and Queen would come and kiss them goodnight, and the King always had something in his pocket for them.

"I know one should not criticize people like that, but it is *not* right," said Mrs Bill, and she was sticking to that one.

When the royal pair returned from their exhausting tour of 1901 (oh, how the Princess had been looking forward to it!) and they had to make a public drive through the crowded streets from Waterloo to Buckingham Palace, London had dressed itself up for them. Waterloo looked magnificent and, as they drove out into the street, they received what was said to be the biggest reception that royalty had ever had.

In truth the country loved young blood. People had grown tired of the brave old widowed Queen whom they never saw, and who mouldered her life away in the Island. They were delighted to see that may-blossom complexion of Princess May again, her smile, and Georgy's salute! Edward VII had brought a tremendous thrill to the throne with him.

But, as the Princess said, "I never knew that there would be so much to do."

It meant, of course, that she saw less and less of her children and she hated this. Preparing for the coronation of her parents-in-law was a big task, but she prepared properly because she was that sort of person. "I shall be so glad when it is all over," she wrote to a friend.

The hour was near, and now the street decorations and stands began to go up. At Marlborough House the children were intensely excited about it all. During the years of mourning

Victoria had always refused to have decorations of any sort, and London had missed the thrill. Now here were the strings of bays, the great branches of leaves, and the gay lights.

"The whole thing is a most tremendous effort," the Princess of Wales wrote, "one hardly dare think how one will get through it."

On 15th June when every village, even my father's tiny parish in the Cotswolds, was preparing for the great day, the news leaked out that the King was not well. After all, he was no longer a young man. It was Ascot Week and the Royal Family were at Windsor, doing it in style as in the old days before the Court had been plunged into that eternal mourning.

Apparently the King was in great pain, and the cause was given out as lumbago. On the 24th of the month, another opinion was called in, for Edward was worse. Now the previous diagnosis was ruled out and we were told that it was not lumbago at all but a new complaint known as appendicitis. It was said to be extremely dangerous, and meant an immediate, *most risky* operation.

Everything was abandoned in a moment, and the men worked all night in the streets to get the decorations down again, for it would be a ghastly thing if the King died, and his funeral had to be through *decorated* streets!

The Princess of Wales was deeply worried for she was devoted to her father-in-law, who would do anything for her, and had helped her enormously and always so willingly, even if he *was* something of a nuisance with spoiling the children.

The King was taken back to Buckingham Palace, and enormous crowds were there. It seemed too dreadful to have waited all these years for him to come to the throne, and he had already changed the whole country to an air of gaiety. Now, if he died, what would happen next?

One can imagine what the Prince and Princess of Wales felt about it. May said that she knew too little to come to the throne, she could not possibly do it. It was a terrible thought! A devout silence had come to London, which had been so joyful before. It was very very much God *save* the King!

My parents were furious, especially my father, who said it was so maddening to have waited all these years for a good king (like Edward was) to come to the throne. He had never been so mad about Victoria, and always said she lost her head when Prince Albert died, and should have abdicated then so that her son could reign.

When eventually the news got through that the operation had been a success, and that the King would live, London went mad. We did not in the country, for we were still wondering what to do with all that food we had got in for a village beano! Crowds surged around the palace, but they were very quiet, for none wished to disturb the royal patient.

It must have been a tremendous relief to the Princess of Wales, who had been waiting there for the news and always said it was one of the darkest hours of her whole life! Poor lady! She little knew how many dark hours lay before her, for rarely did a princess or a queen go through a harder time than she did.

There is the story that Prince David begged to see his grandfather, and eventually was told he could be taken to his room, but he must be a very good boy. He behaved marvellously (his first visit to a sick room; always before this it had been seeing Mamma when she had produced a new brother or sister). Then, when leaving, he asked if he could see the new baby. Unfortunately this quite innocent inquiry very nearly burst the King's stitches, for he laughed so much!

The King was slow in recovering, and in the end an abbreviated coronation was suggested for him. London recovered its gaiety. There were children playing in the gardens of Marlborough House, including a young heir to the throne. It was no longer a tired old Queen who had practically put herself into exile, and a middle-aged Prince and Princess of Wales waiting year after year for their turn to come, but a new generation.

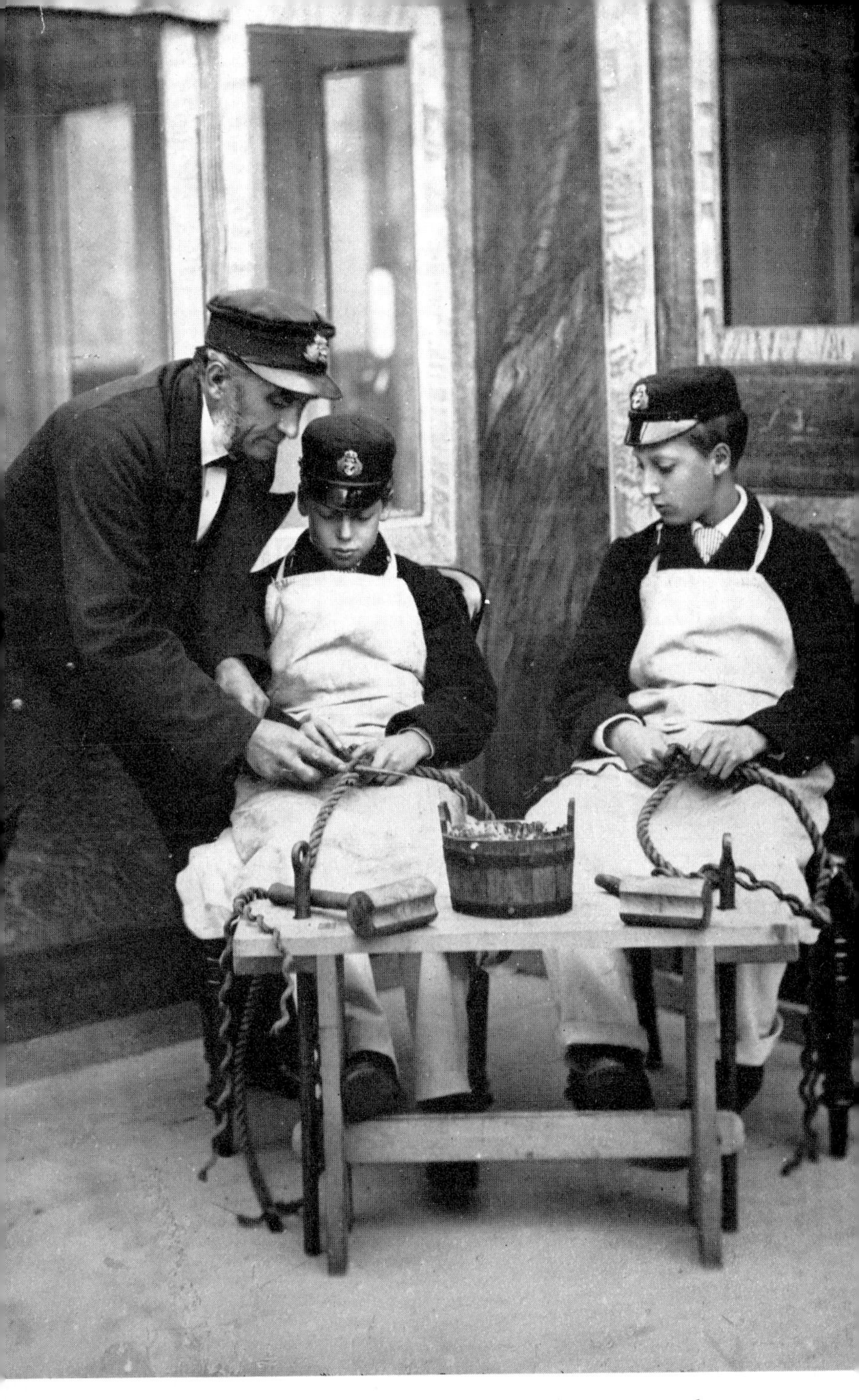

The future King George V and the Duke of Clarence as cadets

left: The Duke of Clarence *right*: The Duke of York, later King George V

The Princess of Wales enjoyed the newly awakened London. Theatres did well. The music hall was the vogue, there were cheap seats, and very thrilling turns to watch, glorious girls to be seen as well. Frequently the Prince and Princess of Wales were to be seen in the royal box.

"It's a new world, and a good one," said the people.

The Princess of Wales enjoyed the newly awakened London. patronized everything that she could, but her one worry was that the children could not bicycle in the gardens of her home. There were far too many rockeries for this, and she felt that someone must have adored rockeries to put in so many.

She had suffered tortures when the King had had his sudden appendix operation, and although she said as little as possible, it had been sheer horror. She had to be ready to become Queen overnight, and she knew that she was far from prepared for this.

She wrote to a friend:

> As yet I really know so little about it, and there is such a tremendous lot to learn.

When the coronation took place, the ceremonial was very much reduced, for the King could not have stood the full service. There were decorations of course, but everything had to be done to make it simpler for His Majesty, who did not recover his strength as quickly as his doctors had hoped.

But time would help him, and he had come down a little in weight, which pleased the Queen and his doctors.

As has been seen, the Princess of Wales busied herself with changing Marlborough House. Queen Alexandra's time of occupation coincided with the era of ill-matching furniture, innumerable matterless ornaments, a flood of photographs in silver frames (Lallie Charles was *the* photographer of the day), and every room was over-furnished. No doubt the Nineties had been a time of the worst possible taste in the home.

The Princess was expert at re-arrangement. But in her personal appearance she very much adhered to the same clothes that she had always worn and, under her husband's influence, did not follow the fashion with other women. This was a mistake. When she had been a young girl she had been so radiant, but now she adhered to over-trimmed dresses touching the ground. She preferred a rather severe type for day wear, in the place of the 'pretty-pretties' that her mother-in-law had always worn. Although on state occasions sometimes she wore remarkably beautiful evening dresses, ordinarily her taste was unattractive.

Ahead of her in 1905 lay a long tour (to India), when she and the Prince would be away for several months, and the thought of separation from the children agonized her. Gone were the good old days when she played tip-and-run with them at Sandringham, or danced a reel with Prince George at Balmoral. She said that being Princess of Wales made tremendous demands on one.

She set forth rather sadly (and she dare not show this) on one of those exacting journeys which were part of her official duty, leaving in the October, to return the following April. It seemed to her to be for ever! "The children will have grown up when I come back, and I shall hardly know them, they will have altered so much," and sadly: "*I* shall have changed also."

Men accept this sort of thing more readily; the Prince took it far better than she did, as he was born to it. By nature the Princess was tenderly sympathetic, her own home life had been spent in the bosom of her family, and she fretted that she could not bring up her own children in the same way.

Mrs Bill was left in charge. Again a large map was pegged to the schoolroom wall, with a little flag pinned to it showing every day where their parents were at that hour.

Apart from missing the children, the Princess of Wales felt very low for another reason: she was not a good sailor. She enjoyed seeing the world, but she admitted that nothing stopped you being seasick, or getting most desperately tired, and one dare not show it for a moment. "You have to appear happy and at ease," she said. "Not so simple when you are seasick!"

On this occasion she confessed that she had never been so tired in her life. Even the Prince of Wales said that it was 'a bit much at times'. But they did their duty and in due course they returned, much to her joy.

The Princess was on deck when the hazy first sight of her own country came on to the horizon (she had asked to be summoned from below for this) and she rose and fell on her toes, as she always did when she was thrilled.

She had never thought that the children would look so much older. Prince Henry, the fourth child, was the tall one. The homecoming was a real thrill. They had managed to bring home glorious gifts for them.

"Not too many at a time," said Mrs Bill, warningly.

After this, the Princess had a short period of relaxation, which she had not been able to get on the tour. There it had been impossible because something was always happening, too many engagements were made for them, engagements which demanded tremendous efforts, but now they were home again and she *could* relax.

She played with the children again, wandered out into the gardens with them, and she said that they were the greatest tonic that she could have.

"It is so good to be home," she said.

4

Queen

But relaxation can never last for very long with a Queen-to-be. In 1909 the Prince and Princess of Wales had to attend the marriage of Princess Victoria Eugenie (Ena) of Battenberg to the young King of Spain. Alfonso had come to England in search of a queen. King Edward was a discreet matchmaker, and he had his eye on Princess Patricia of Connaught as a suitable bride. But Patricia did not rise to the bait; in fact she failed to turn up at an introductory palace ball.

The King of Spain was a most difficult guest, because he was out for fun! He would slip out and hail a common-or-garden taxi, saying to the cabby, "Take me somewhere interesting." One taximan asked if he was not the King of Spain, and he said, "Yes, I am, but don't tell anybody. I don't want a fuss!" The man took him up Bond Street, where he was recognized and had to slip away down a side street and run for another taxi. King Edward, always a most understanding man, laughed. "He wants his fun, and he isn't likely to get it in Spain. Let him have a spree here," he said.

Alfonso certainly did not miss Princess Patricia at the palace ball, for, being very susceptible, he fell for the fair-haired, very pretty Princess Ena of Battenberg. He had a passion for fair hair; he paid her delicate compliments and kept on dancing with her all night.

Edward VII was quite happy about it.

King Alfonso sent his love a most attractive little orange tree in a pot. The tree was laden with oranges. He also gave her rare jewels. They each fell in love with the other (everyone was charmed over the royal romance), they went about together, and on one occasion they went down to Windsor, and he adored it. They became engaged.

King Edward arranged his princesses admirably. Ena had to learn Spanish, and take instruction in the Roman Catholic faith.

At her wedding, a madman – the anarchist Morales – flung a bomb which nearly killed them. How they escaped, nobody will ever know. The Prince and Princess of Wales were travelling four carriages behind the King of Spain's, and May said that it was one of the most ghastly moments of her life. She never knew how she faced the subsequent State lunch or (if it came to that) how anyone did! It was certainly one of the most dreadful moments of poor Princess Mary's life. "A most unpleasant experience," she wrote. She was never more thankful to get back to Marlborough House and her children.

King Edward was more worldly-minded than his aged mother had been. "Life is so different with him, and he is such a very kind man," his daughter-in-law said, and this was true.

In the gayer, Edwardian London her children were growing up, and she did not seem to have as much time for them. It was far more difficult to be their mother now that she was Princess of Wales, but she always looked forward to going to Scotland in August, for there they could all lead a more countrified life. She practised reels with her sons, and she went for long country walks with them, for she had always shared the old Queen's dedication to Balmoral.

Possibly she would have preferred to have been an ordinary wife and mother. She would have given her life to husband and children, but the crown was for ever demanding, and always coming closer. Once she said, "It commands one. It can be quite alarming."

She was a little apprehensive, for she knew that King Edward felt this era of peace would not last for ever. He never had trusted his German nephew, and once had said that one of these days there could be war with Germany which would be disastrous.

For that, among other reasons, he helped to draw Britain closer to France in the *Entente Cordiale*.

The Princess of Wales had, at one time, been anxious lest the King might have thought of one of the Kaiser's daughters as a bride for her eldest son, David. Her husband, guessing her thoughts, had said, "All mothers worry about whom their sons will marry, and more so about the eldest one!" He had thought one had to leave these things to fate. She said, at the time, "But I don't think she would be the right wife for him. I've never cared for her father too much."

The Prince had laughed. "Who *has*?" he asked.

She felt that somehow men seldom understand the workings of a woman's mind. She knew that her eldest son would have to make what she felt was a marriage for the state; this is the fate of princes, and rather naturally it worried her.

"Let's wait and see what happens," her husband suggested, and she had to let it be.

In Spain Queen Ena had a son, and the news came very joyfully to England for the young Queen had done the right thing. Only a short time later, it transpired that the child was a haemophiliac, as one of her uncles had been, an infection carried through the women of the family. Spain was furious with her for it!

She had a second son next year, and he was born what the nurses called deaf and dumb. Prince Jaime. Could anything have been worse? For now the country, wildly superstitious, declared that the hand of fate was against the royal couple, and I dare say King Alfonso himself (who had not too amiable a temper when roused) was none too nice over it.

The poor Queen had a daughter next time. Then another son, but he was born dead. Just before his birth Edward VII died. There was nothing that did not go wrong for her. Her fourth son was another 'bleeder'.

I believe that during her earlier trials King Edward wrote her the most comforting letters, which helped her, and she always said that he was the nicest uncle for any girl to have. But her marriage had fallen apart.

Alfonso himself was volatile, delightful at times, cruel at other moments, and naturally he always wanted his own way and saw that he got it. Naturally with his heir a 'bleeder' and the second son deaf, and almost dumb with it, the people did say that the marriage had been 'doomed'. It was dreadful for Ena.

It had been such a marvellous marriage at first, obviously a love match. Alfonso had made the most magnificent lover, sending her dazzling gifts, quite bewildering in their beauty.

But after the birth of the Prince of the Asturias, of course, things did become different. Nobody had suspected that the child would be a bleeder. In those days one drew a veil over such secrets, which never came out into the open. I very much doubt if Queen Ena had even *known* of the possibility of haemophilia, and naturally it was one of those things never referred to, nor spoken of.

The Princess of Wales was horrified, for although she knew about the presence of haemophilia in Queen Victoria's family, she had never thought of this malady being handed on into her day, for, she said, surely a cure had been found for such a shocking inheritance?

To this day no cure apparently has been found either inside or outside royal circles.

Everything had started off on the wrong foot for the young King and Queen of Spain. When the Princess of Wales mentioned it, her husband said it never did to look too far ahead into the future. We had to live today for today; time enough to worry when their own eldest son got married! She wondered what sort of a queen he would bring into this country, and hoped that she would be a charming girl.

She knew that dear Mrs Bill had always said that David was not as reliable as his brothers, but she adored him, and perhaps excused him too soon. She frolicked with her children, was very good at cricket, praying that David would make the right marriage when the time came, for although she never mentioned it, she did not forget her first love, poor Prince Albert Victor.

She laughed, for life was merry, London was enjoyable, and she adored good theatres and entertainments. There was the first night of *The Merry Widow* in 1907, an unforgettable occasion when the audience went mad.

And she would never forget the tremendous thrill when the King's horse, Minoru, won the Derby, and her father-in-law, stoutening very much, led him in before a crowd that had gone absolutely mad. Possibly that was the greatest thrill of his reign! She felt like a girl again. It was good to be enjoying herself, and so happy.

There was now a lot of talk about the King and Mrs Keppel, Lady Warwick, and others, and everybody knew that he had not been his mother's favourite son, but he was a man you could not help loving. Once, at Warwick Castle, he gave Maynard Greville and myself, aged about six at the time, half a crown and said, "Slip out and get yourselves as many sweets as you can, and don't tell anybody I told you so."

Everyone loved him, and his daughter-in-law was devoted to him.

But the King was putting on too much weight. He had inherited stoutness from his mother, not his father, who stayed fairly slender to the end. But the King liked good food, he liked the pleasures of life, and did not heed too much what his doctors told him.

He went off to Biarritz (one of his favourite resorts) in the spring of 1910, saying that he was tired and could do with a breath of fair France. It was April (always a fickle month) and the weather was none too good for him, though he would never have admitted this, for he swore by Biarritz and would not hear a word said against it.

"I do hope that he isn't really ill," the Princess of Wales said, when the news came that he had a cold.

Apparently he could not shake it off, but, recovering a little, he felt that he was well enough to make the journey home, which he did. When he got back to the palace Queen Alexandra was shocked to see how ill he looked, and obviously *was*. The doctors took a serious outlook of his condition. He worsened.

It was then that Queen Alexandra made one of those intuitive decisions that she so often did, for she was a woman who always seemed to understand the other person's viewpoint. She sent for his best friend, Mrs Keppel, and explained her action to one of her ladies-in-waiting, with the four simple words: "I want *his* happiness!"

England was not prepared for the seriousness of his condition. The end came for us – with unexpected suddenness. The postman, going his early rounds on the morning of 6th May told us that the King was dead. The Prince and Princess of Wales had been at Buckingham Palace since the previous afternoon, and were with him when he died.

The Princess of Wales had gone to his room with fear in her heart. It brought back memories of the day at Sandringham when she (engaged to Prince Albert Victor) had knelt beside his bed and had seen him die. She stood back from the others, now gathered round Edward VII, with the dreadful feeling in her heart: *This has happened before*. She saw the moment when others kissed her husband's hand, and she knew, to her own cold horror, when they kissed hers that she was Queen of England.

It was with the greatest difficulty that she stopped herself from fainting, and turned to comfort her mother-in-law. Queen Alexandra was amazingly courageous about it. Queen Mary would never forget how brave she was.

"It ... it has happened ..." the new Queen gasped, aghast and dismayed, and she wept.

He had been the kindest father-in-law that any woman could ever have, she always said, someone she could trust implicitly, and the best of men, and she wept bitterly.

She had a dreadful premonition that at this moment the England built up so nobly by Queen Victoria, pulled out of the chaos in which the Hanoverians had left it, was suddenly going for ever! An entirely new world lay round the corner. She was filled with alarm. There had always been moments in her life when she had seen clearly ahead, and she was afraid. From the instant that Edward VII ceased breathing the world changed. She felt apprehensive, even afraid.

"I have lost my best friend," she said with truth.

One of her younger sons, when he heard of it, burst into tears and said, "Now there is nobody to play bears with me!"

Somehow she associated the two remarks – her best friend, and nobody to play bears!

5

Royal Tours and Duties

There was the usual prolonged tremendous funeral and Queen Alexandra seemed to have become strangely small as she stood behind her husband's bier. Queen Mary wept for her, for herself also – for now her life would be full and there would be no Sandringham, for this was left to the Queen Mother. Queen Mary had hardly seen her husband since the King died, so it seemed. He wrote of his father:

> I never had a word with him in my life. I am heart-broken.

And this she knew was probably true of everyone who knew him, for he had been the most charming man, and always so understanding.

The Queen felt a sense of sudden loneliness when she came to the throne, as though she had shut out a world she loved. When alone, she wept. Homeliness had gone; she was now the woman who wore the crown.

"Everything has changed far too much," she told Mrs Bill, who understood her. Mrs Bill said that later on it would be easier, she must give herself time. But in her heart she knew that this did not happen to queens. Things do not right themselves.

She went to Scotland in that summer of 1910. There she felt even worse, for her second brother, Prince Francis of Teck, had had a most unpleasant operation, recovered a little, and then unexpectedly collapsed and died at the age of thirty-nine. It was the first loss of her own generation, something she had not expected, for all her brothers were younger than herself. She broke down at the funeral (the only time in her life), and later she said: "I just don't know what happened to me."

Her husband said: "It happens to all of us at some time," and she remembered that he had lost *his* brother, she kneeling by Eddy's bedside, something that she could never forget, try as she would. She admitted that the start to their reign was not a very happy one. She had overworked, and the throne demanded more of her than ever before.

The grief was that now she would not be going down to Sandringham, for the cottage was too small, and the Queen Mother was at the big house. She supposed that she would settle to the new life in time, but for the moment it worried her, and the strain of a coronation lying ahead of her was something that she hardly dared think about.

She supposed that, given time, she would be happier, but there were so many things to do that it made her feel that she had left the great happinesses of her life behind her, the children young, and she playing cricket with them at York Cottage. "I adored York Cottage," she said once in an outburst of homesickness for it.

It must have been about now (a very hot summer) that the faint rumour of a coming war was heard. She did not believe that it could be true; surely, with advanced civilization, we had outgrown wars? Who would dare fight us, with the greatest army in the world, and the valiant new dreadnoughts on the sea?

"But surely war would never come?" she asked her husband. "I mean it would be madness, surely?"

He was not so sure. The whisper was everywhere, and he personally suspected his German cousin, who, he said, believed could do anything! Seeing her anxiety, he said the thing to do was to live for today, and in a way this comforted her. Privately he did not think war would come, for we were a very big power.

Before the coronation he silenced a rumour that had been going about for twenty years (I heard it as a child, from the parlour-maid in her pantry). It was that George had married the daughter of an English admiral when he was very young, stationed at Malta, and his marriage to Queen Mary was therefore non-existent. The story first appeared in the *Star* newspaper in 1893. After the King's accession a journalist, Edward Mylius, revived the *canard* in a Paris sheet, *The Liberator*. The King sued for libel. How anyone dared put this into print I cannot imagine, but in a fit of daring (or malice) they *did*, and this gave the King a chance to clear up something which had been worrying him for ages.

During the famous case which followed it transpired, of course, that this was mere gossip. The King had not been stationed in Malta at the time of this supposed illegal marriage, and the whole story was untrue.

I think that our servants at home were very disappointed with the outcome of this, but Queen Mary must have been very thankful to get it cleared up for ever. At times it had been quite unpleasant, and she felt that the thing to do was to stop it at the start of their reign, which they did.

"Now that will end," she said with relief, and to him: "So ridiculous when you were never in the island, what dreadful tales people do circulate about us, given the chance."

She prepared for the coronation.

"I'm awfully nervous," she told him.

He asked in his blunt way, "Who wouldn't be?" His father had told him it was the hardest day's work that he had ever had. The Queen wrote to a friend:

> I am tired to death with it all. Oh, how deeply I regret leaving dear Marlborough House, the most perfect of all houses ...

Queen Mary was a woman who got very attached to her backgrounds, and she loathed an upheaval. But the tiresome plans for the coronation continued. Six daughters of earls would carry her train (as was the rule) and the service would follow the accepted pattern. It had only been abbreviated for the late King because he was insufficiently restored from his operation to stand too much.

In this summer of 1911 the good weather began on Good

Friday, and was the start to a most amazing summer. There was something like an Easter heat-wave, and this went on almost to the day of the coronation. The sun was ever in the sky; then, just before the coronation, it disappeared! On the actual day it was quite chilly (intensified by the previous heat). People waited in the streets all night, with sandwiches, and hot tea and coffee barrows being pushed up and down before them. But it was horribly cold, compared to the earlier weather.

The royal pair left the palace dead on time in the golden coach and came out of the gates to tremendous cheering, which the Queen said helped her. Prince George was the most elated person, bouncing up and down in the seat of the coach carrying the royal children, trying to see everything both sides at the same minute. The crowd loved it. Prince George was such a nuisance that his two elder brothers put him under the seat in the end, and when they got back Mrs Bill thought they had come home one short!

They all enjoyed the coronation save the Prince of Wales, who was nervous and worried. That night the Queen wrote of him: "David looked charming in his purple and miniver cloak and gold circlet.

The King wrote in *his* diary with very real affection about her:

> Dear May looked so elegant. It was comforting to have her by my side, as she has been during the last eighteen years.

She herself had turned very nervous, and admitted it. At heart she was still shy, something which she always had to cover up, as she put it, "if only for other people's sakes", and she tried to hide her reserve with a smile. She knew she would never have a moment to herself again, for the crown would demand everything of her.

She was now forty-six years old, and showing every sign of putting on weight, which worried her, and she ate with caution, not easy at public functions. She said to a friend: "The engagements take hours of every day. I'm always changing my

Queen Mary's homes: *top*: White Lodge, Richmond Park, where she was brought up; York Cottage, Sandringham, where Queen Mary lived in the early days of her marriage; Sandringham, King George V's favourite home; *bottom*: Marlborough House, London, home when Queen Mary became Princess of Wales

The Prince and Princess of Wales' wedding photograph

dress, and usually against time, which is *not* amusing."

Home, the children, the garden, and all those things which once had been an all-absorbing part of her life, seemed to have faded. "Crowns take up too much of one's life, too much time," she said, sadly.

She was a strong woman physically and did not tire easily, and could manage to show the world a brave face, but she did find there was a tremendous lot to do. Queen Alexandra had warned her that crowns were heavy, but she never thought they would be as heavy as this.

When on coronation night she went to bed after stepping continually on to the palace balcony and waving to the crowds, she told her ladies that she had never been quite so tired before! I should think that this was true. A queen has too much to do.

Each day for the rest of the week the newly crowned monarchs drove into the suburbs so that people who could not get to the coronation would get a chance to see them. This, too, was extremely fatiguing, and took a lot of time.

Then she had to start to prepare for something more exhausting – a second visit to India, this time for the Durbar. She had never been particularly good in hot weather, felt the heat badly, and, growing stouter, did not relish the prospect. On the tour she was to wear, one day, all her coronation robes, heavy and extremely hot, of course. But she was not one of those people who spare themselves.

She loathed leaving her children again. But the tour was essential: George V and Queen Mary were the first reigning monarchs jointly to receive the homage, directly and personally, of the peoples and the rulers of the Indian states.

The heat proved to be much worse than she had anticipated. The Emperor and Empress of India were to make a state entry, as was expected of them, on elephants, which had the advantage of raising the visitors high up so that everyone on the route in Delhi could see them. "Not that I am too thrilled about the thought of riding on an *elephant*," she said when plans were being discussed.

But for some reason these plans were changed.

The Emperor himself entered the city on horseback, which was not at all a good idea, for there were such enormous crowds assembled there that most of the people never saw him at all. But that was what they wanted. The Empress drove behind him, sitting in an open carriage drawn by six horses.

Later she admitted that she felt "rather nervous".

It was all so very different from the sort of world to which she was accustomed, and the heat *terrible*! The noises the crowd made were like nothing that she had ever heard before, and she could not tell if they were expressive of joy or dismay.

But it turned out to be a most magnificent reception.

As to the celebrations, she classed them as being "the best that I have ever seen, quite wonderful!" She did not care for the reception at which she had to wear her coronation robes, mostly velvet and very hot (the ones in which she had actually been crowned at Westminster), but her Indian subjects wanted this. When they had been made it was for the English climate. "I became aware of *that*," she told one of her ladies with a smile. "I don't know how I got through it!"

She had one horrifying moment, which could have ended in catastrophe, at a reception held in a huge marquee. Suddenly, no one knew how, something caught fire. In the stillness of a very hot country fire moves fast (and it did), but neither George nor Mary flinched. Both had tremendous self-control.

She heard him whisper, "It's all right, May," and knew that he would not have said so if it were not true.

Fire in a hot country is hard to fight, and she saw that flames *did* travel faster than they ever did in England.

But on the whole she enjoyed the Indian visit, and she heard from the children daily, accompanied by constant letters from Mrs Bill herself, who was most understanding of the details that their mother wanted to know.

"I miss them all quite terribly," she said. "That is the worst of the trip, but we all have to put up with something in life, though

I do feel they will all be grown up when I return, and I shall hardly know them."

She was very pleased to hear that Prince Henry had "put a spurt on", as Mrs Bill expressed it.

She could hardly believe it was true when they embarked for home. No more crowds. Time to rest. With every throb of the engine, one heart-beat nearer to the children. "It is," she confessed to her husband, "quite nice not to be on show for a while."

She relaxed a little to recover from the strain, and could take time over everything which was a big help. This is wonderful, she told herself.

But, as they neared home, the weather changed, and she had never thought for a moment how much she would miss the heat. At the time it had seemed to be suffocating, now the journey was like ice! She developed a bad cold, of course, something that almost everybody does on that sort of trip, and oh, how thankful she was when the King showed her that dim blue line of England approaching.

"We can't really be back," she gasped and then, almost in tears, "The *children*!"

The wind was cold, and it was raining when they landed. It was weeks since she had seen rain, and this amazed her. She would never forget meeting the children again. How tall Harry had grown (Mrs Bill had warned her of this). How gay George looked, and the tender kisses of her daughter Mary.

"I've been away too long. They have actually grown up and I was not here to see it," she said, rather regretfully.

There was a lot to be done now that she had got back, and the King was immediately whisked away to work. She dealt with unending letters set aside for her. At one time she thought that she would never 'catch up', but of course she did. She would have given a lot to go down again to the quiet of Sandringham, but there was no room for them there now.

She worried that perhaps the dear old life had gone for ever. The homeliness of playing cricket with the boys, dancing a reel with Georgy, trying to teach her only daughter to sew, something that she herself loved doing. The crown had the power to change everything for her, and she was realizing this.

A special visit North was being planned for the King and Queen. They had not been there for some time, and it was Dr Cosmo Gordon Lang who very much wanted them to go. He drew the King's attention to industrial conditions which, he said, "needed looking into". Living in London, they only got a limited idea of how the North was affected at this time and how dreadfully poor many people were.

The King was most interested in everything that Dr Lang had to tell him, and he thought that it was right: they ought to pay a visit North. Dr Lang said that at the moment many Northerners thought that they were a forgotten people, and this was unfair on them. They worked hard, were intensely poor, some living in hovels, and something ought to be done about it. A royal visit would give the people heart, and make them realize that, even if they thought they were forgotten, they were not.

They went.

The Queen was absolutely shocked by the poverty she saw and the tremendous distress of the people. She went into some of the rather derelict hovels where some of them lived, asking the most sensible questions about how they lived. She wanted to know the cost of living, of food especially, and the wages that their husbands earned. She had always been extremely practical and they recognized this, and appreciated it. One woman asked her: "But how do you *know*, your Majesty?"

She turned and said: "My people were not rich. We had to be very careful at times, and it worried them a lot. I have known about it ever since I was a little girl." How very true!

Of course, she had never been actually hungry, as some of those poor people were, but she remembered when her fiancé died, and the enormous bills for her trousseau were unpaid, all the cold horror that she had felt at the time.

The people took to the Queen in a big way, for she was most sympathetic and understanding with their troubles.

"The King has got a fine upstanding woman for his wife," was what they said about her. "She says as how she will do summut for us."

What she had actually said was that she was not in a position to do anything, but that she would remind the King, and go on reminding him, so that in the end something *would* be done by the government. When she promised them, "I will do everything that I can, because this shocks me", they knew that she meant what she said.

That year they went back to Balmoral, which she had always loved, though Sandringham was her favourite house and, possibly, next to it, York Cottage (poky as it had seemed to be at times). Both of them were working hard. Then, in the June of 1914, suddenly the big tragedy which was to change everybody's life appeared on the horizon.

There had been a ghastly outrage in Europe, in the country which at the time we called Servia. This had always been a turbulent Balkans country (one never expected calmness there), but this time there was the start to something infinitely greater than anything that we had ever had before.

The Archduke Franz Ferdinand of Austria-Hungary and his morganatic wife, the Duchess of Hohenberg, were driving through Sarajevo when both of them were shot dead by an assassin. They were going through the formalities of a state visit when this happened; both were killed outright.

When the news flashed across the world, Queen Mary was positively stunned by it, for she had the hideous foreboding that this was not the end of an interlude, but the beginning of something quite terrible. She was, of course, right.

"I have a ghastly feeling about it," she told her husband.

He said this sort of thing had happened before, and so often in that neighbourhood, and it had not done too much, so far. She was most unhappy about it. "Those three children that they had, what has happened to the children? Oughtn't something to be done for them?" she asked.

The King said they would be cared for. Men take these things more calmly, of course. It was not the first time there had been some assassination out there.

It seemed, for a short while, as if nothing very much had happened after all, though the newspapers made comments, and there was a general state of uneasiness throughout Europe. The season ended, and the Royal Family went to the Isle of Wight for the famous Cowes Week. But the Queen was quite right in the horror that she had felt, and the doubt. We were on the verge of a world war.

Of course there had been murders of foreign royals before this, nothing much had happened afterwards, and the scandal had died down. One thought of the Portuguese tragedy when the King and the Crown Prince were both killed in a very similar attack when driving through the streets, and that had shocked the world.

The Queen recalled her own experiences on the day of the marriage of King Alfonso and Queen Ena in Madrid, when she had been but a stone's throw from the bomb explosion, an experience she would never forget! She had the horrible foreboding that this trouble in Servia was not going to be settled as easily as at first they had thought.

Before we knew where we were, the news in the papers was foreboding. Queen Mary was most unhappy about it, for she could not convince herself that all would be well, as many others seemed to think.

As Cowes Week drew to its close, the Fleet left as had been arranged, going on to Torbay for the Royal Review. It was from there that Winston Churchill, then First Lord of the Admiralty, ordered it to sea to a destination unknown – the famous Fleet mobilization at Scapa Flow.

This was the first time when the man-in-the-street suddenly

and quite clearly became aware of something serious going on, something that he did not quite understand. The Queen was horrified, for she knew earlier with messengers coming and going all the time, and she realized that the crisis was rapidly becoming dangerous.

We were, of course, a great and powerful nation with the finest fleet in the world, and we had no apprehension that anything could go really wrong. But all wars mean death and destruction and these, she must have known, could be around the next bend. The King would have told her little, certainly she would never have asked him, but her ladies noticed that she was quieter, and more unhappy than she had been for a long time.

She wrote to a friend that she found this a very anxious time, and only hoped that there were better times ahead. She knew, of course, the old story which had gone the rounds that Kaiser Wilhelm II thought that because he was the eldest son of Queen Victoria's eldest child he should inherit the throne of England! He had always disliked King Edward VII, who had 'taken his place' as he put it, and his uncle had thought very little of him. She must have prayed for no war.

Already it seemed that the life around her was changing. In war, she said, too many die, too many are injured and left to suffer. It can never be easy.

War was declared at midnight on 4th August 1914, and an immense crowd surged round Buckingham Palace shrieking with joy, for they all said this would teach that cocky German emperor something! But the Queen was most fearful. It would not be the short war that everybody anticipated, weeks travel quickly into months when there is a war on; she was praying for a short war, which most of us believed it *must* be, because nobody could stand up to British might for long, but we forgot that the South African war had dragged on long after anyone had anticipated, and a European war *could* be worse.

We believed that our troops would be eating their Christmas dinners in Berlin. But did the Queen think this? I doubt it.

The King himself was appalled by the Kaiser's brazen actions. He said that he was stuck-up, and now he saw that he was taking a giant risk in the hope of winning England for himself.

"But it won't come off," said the King.

That comforted the Queen a little, for she knew that King George had never been a wildly optimistic man, and it was consoling that he was sure of winning this war. This was August, the last summer month for a world which, until this hour, had been at peace. One hardly dare look ahead.

Her first homely tasks were knitting for the troops, for we were close to the coming winter, and they would want good scarves, waistcoats and jerseys. She was always extremely practical in her outlook and she ordered strict retrenchment in the palaces. When the cold weather came the big rooms were icy, and she envied the hospitals which had good fires to warm them. She said to one hospital matron: "It's lovely here! You don't know how awfully cold Buckingham Palace is, and I think Windsor is worse! We almost have to *sit* on the fires to keep ourselves warm."

She turned to the material side of the work. She had loved needlework from childhood, knitted well, and impressed on her helpers that no time must be lost.

That was the most gruelling winter, a dreadful enlightenment to most of us as to how we had sat back, and how vastly other nations had improved in more modern warfare. The long lists of casualties were ghastly. The Queen had been quite right in her anxiety for the immediate future. The Kaiser had a vast army prepared, and, by the end of October, we had given up any idea of the war being over by Christmas. The Queen had never thought that would be possible. She was quite sure that the Kaiser would never have started the fight if he had not been well prepared for it himself. He must have been planning this for years.

She went out to France, wanting to visit the hospitals there in person, though the experience upset her quite dreadfully. Her sympathetic nature made things worse.

"I've got to do everything that I *can* do to help," she said to her own ladies. "It is no good pushing on other people, then standing back yourself. I have *got* to go."

It was a most bitter venture and once, after visiting a big hospital, she had to wipe away her tears and then she admitted: "I just can't get accustomed to seeing suffering. It actually hurts me. The awful part is that I can't help them really, and it is so ghastly when they are all so *young*."

The needlework guilds that she organized comforted her, for they covered the world, and one day in the country when I was walking her car passed me and she and one of her ladies were sitting there knitting as they went along! In the first years of the war she must have organized the most tremendous output of knitting for the troops that there had ever been. But she was worried to death, for the whole war had been so much worse than she had ever anticipated.

The King visited the front when he could, and when he was away he and the Queen wrote daily to one another. Love had ripened, and they cared devotedly for each other. All the time she had the most ominous feeling that "something would happen to him", and, when he was away, she was desperately depressed.

"I get silly ideas," she told one of her ladies, who knew this was the way that she felt. "It is so tiresome, for however hard I try to stop it I fail!"

All her life she had been apprehensive of what she called "silly ideas one gets", and this was a very insistent one, increased, she believed, because of the cloud of war which hung over everyone. Perhaps all women felt this way when their husbands went overseas. Curiously, she did not feel half so worried for her David, the young Prince of Wales who was serving in France, as she did for her husband who only paid France flying visits.

It was the Prince of Wales himself who had insisted on going overseas, and he did not ask to have extra protection. His mother had agreed that he was right in wishing to go, and almost every woman of her age had a son fighting overseas, why should *her* son stay behind because he was heir to the throne? she asked. "I have plenty of brothers" – that was what *he* said.

The King was kept busy; much was demanded of him, and whenever he was at the Front she was curiously distressed. She was, of course, sure that every care would be taken of him, and no risks run, yet from the first she had been so sure that some day, some time, something would happen.

"But that is only natural. In war every mother and every wife must be worried."

She aged more with the anxiety. It was a wretched time, and everyone was worried. The war seemed to be going on for ever.

In the spring of 1915 one still believed the year would see the end of the war. Now here they were in the October of 1917 – the year in which she was first allowed to visit Flanders – and as yet there was no sign of peace being even within sight.

On that occasion she recalled a brilliant autumn afternoon in 1915 when she went for a drive in Windsor Park, at the time of year when all the leaves were turning and it really was very beautiful. She took an old friend with her, and the colour of the trees and bushes was remarkable and somehow one did not think that winter was round the next corner. They admired it very much, talked together, and she felt quite happy. When they returned to Windsor Castle, news was awaiting the Queen's return, and instinctively she knew that something dreadful had happened!

All through the war she had been on edge with the ghastly apprehension that one day the war would hit her own family, and she had prayed that it would not be her son.

"But then," as she said to the friend to whom she had spoken of this, "possibly every woman feels the same way. That is only natural."

At the castle she was informed that the King had suffered an accident in France. Apparently his horse had suddenly shied at a parade at Hesdigneul and had fallen with him. Instantly she recognized it as being what she had feared from the start.

Of course it had been a miracle that the King's life had been saved, and she listened with complete outward calm to the news, for she was a woman who could always keep control of herself. The horse had rolled on him twice. As yet they were not sure of what harm had been done. It was serious, but not the worst that she had always feared. When they told her she said, "You are sure that is all? You are not keeping anything from me?"

"No, your Majesty, and this is true." There was a pause. "There was some strange noise and the horse got alarmed, reared and fell, unseating the King."

In a low voice, but still calm, the Queen said, "He is not dead, and you are trying to break it to me gently?"

She was told that the King was alive, but he was injured. She telephoned to headquarters immediately, and the man she spoke to was the Prince of Wales. It was a real joy to hear his voice. He said that his father had been rolled on twice, and was badly hurt, but not dangerously so. Nothing had been broken, the doctors assured him at first, but some doctor made a bad mistake for the pelvis was broken.

"Can he return, or do I come to him?" she asked.

Her son told her to stay in London for the King would be back in two days, and the Prince himself was coming over next day to tell her about it, which he did.

When eventually the King arrived they found that his pelvis was broken (otherwise it was not too bad), but he had much pain.

Queen Mary had the most superb self-control.

"It is futile to get worried when one can do nothing to help," she once said, and she never lost her head in an emergency, nor did she show any deep emotion when something like this happened, but privately she *was* desperately worried.

The King was a very strong man but he had been working unbelievably hard, much too hard, of course, and he *was* getting older. Her calm often gave the impression that she did not really care, which was quite untrue for deep down within her she got worried to death.

The King returned to the home doctors, whom she trusted implicitly. As he was not dangerously ill, she told him that all along she had had this premonition that something would happen. Every year of the war she had been expecting it, and was now almost glad that the suspense was over.

I always feel that the King never completely recovered from that accident (his official biographer says he was never the same again) because always after he seemed to tire far more easily, with sudden attacks of fatigue, but, of course, he had sons who now could take his place.

"And now he is *home*," said the Queen, ecstatically rising and falling on her toes. "He is home, and that is what matters."

Unfortunately, Germany had been far better prepared for this war than we had thought possible when hostilities had begun. Then we had been sure that no country could stand up to Britain's might, and we were entirely wrong.

Rations were with us (it was far better in the Second World War, when we were more organized). The first war with Germany had come as an utter surprise, and now the casualty lists were appalling. Even worse for the Queen was the fact that as time went on she saw too many of the European crowns falling, and many of her own relatives were in very real distress.

Before 1914 England had been divided into social classes, into which one slipped automatically and which, at the time, we had thought could never change. But it was beginning to change even now.

I remember my horror (recently married to a young captain) when the 'tween-maid' was visited by her young man (who was a major), and my husband, being only a captain, had to call him 'Sir', which my husband very much disliked.

It was a ghastly war, and by the first Christmas the good regiments, which took the first full blow, were just mowed down; the rest of the war seemed to lie in the hands of the

Volunteers and the Territorials.

In her letters to Lady Mountbatten, in 1917, the Queen, much troubled, wrote:

> It is so dreadful, but the war seems to get worse the longer it lasts.

It was that year that the King wrote to the Queen possibly one of the most beautifully expressed letters that he ever penned, which shows quite a different side of his character:

> I can't ever sufficiently express my thanks to you, my darling, for the splendid way in which you are helping me through these terrible times ... If it wasn't for you, I should break down.

She was a wonderful woman in the manner that she could support anyone through a crisis, and few people recognized the way that she never tired, and was absolutely always there to help others. She had already had the most difficult life with the loss of her fiancé, dying as he had done, and she standing behind Queen Alexandra, and living through what must have been the most ghastly experience for any girl. Then, sharing the horror that her parents were almost penniless with buying the trousseau, which she then thought she would never want. But she had married Prince George, though he was not the easiest man in all the world to live with, and she knew it. The Prince of Wales could be a difficult boy, and, of course, she was always deeply worried for her youngest son, little Prince John, who died at Sandringham 18th January 1919.

He was the most charming little boy. Mrs Bill showed me letters he sent her. Just the message ...

> Nannie,
> I love you
> Johnnie.

and she spoke with tears in her eyes about him.

Walking back from church that morning, the King and Queen had called in at the farm where he lived in isolation with Mrs Bill. He had had a shocking attack of epilepsy early that morning, and was only semi-conscious. He was dead before his parents got back over the park to Sandringham House.

The Queen wrote a long letter to a friend about it and in it she said:

> To him it is a great release, for his malady became worse as he grew older. He has thus been spared much suffering. I cannot say how grateful we feel to God for having taken him in such a peaceful way. He just slept quietly into his heavenly home. No pain, no struggle. Just peace for the poor little troubled spirit which had been a great anxiety to us for many years, ever since he was 4 years old.

She could write very beautiful letters to people, for she was such a charming woman. On the night after her only daughter Princess Mary was married, she wrote to the Prince of Wales:

> Papa and I feel very low and said without her, poor Papa broke down, but I mercifully managed to keep up, as I so much feared that Mary would break down, but she was very brave.

When the crowd saw all the rollicking guests in the courtyard of Buckingham Palace, the confetti, the cheers, and the fun that it all seemed to be, little did they imagine that inside, where the farewell took place, this was what had been happening.

For a time after that the King was quite miserable.

6

Bertie's Marriage and a Future Queen

The world was asking the question, *whom will the Prince of Wales marry*? He had grown up far more obstinate than he had been under Mrs Bill in the good old nursery days, for she would stand no rot. Surely the Prince of Wales must marry soon, we sall said.

Then, to our great surprise, it was Princess Mary who became engaged, and she was going to marry a very rich man who was a great deal older than she.

Her fiancé was Viscount Lascelles; he was the future Earl of Harewood, and a millionaire. He was not an attractive man (old enough to be her father), but people said that she adored her father and, because of this, preferred older men.

The Queen seemed to be pleased and, of course, after the stark horrors of war England was enchanted with the thought of a royal wedding. The Marys of England contributed for a gift, and there were thousands of them. We were all trying to go back to the peace that we had known in 1914, little realizing that in life you *cannot* go back.

"It can never be the same," the Queen wrote to a friend, "but to be out of the war is everything. Oh, I am so thankful that it is all over!"

She had taken the suffering of her country very much to heart, and this was, of course, the moment when a royal marriage would give us something thrilling and interesting to talk about. England thought that the bridegroom was "rather old for her" (I have often wondered what his private response to that was). A horde of the most magnificent wedding gifts were on show at St James's Palace, with a queue waiting to see them, stretching right out into the park almost all day.

I have questioned how the Queen felt about this marriage, and parting with her only daughter. She would have said nothing. She had the most brilliant gift for arranging such ceremonies, and she went to the Abbey to inspect it privately. She had got the idea that this would be far more suitable for royal weddings than any other place. And, with the big open surrounds, thousands more of the public would get the chance to see it.

The Abbey had a very long nave, more guests could be invited; it had, in fact, everything.

When the day came – 28th February 1922 – the little bride was quite pathetically nervous. She had always been a very shy child, Mrs Bill had told me, hating what Mrs Bill called 'showing off', so she would not have been too happy.

Thousands waited to greet her as, with her father, she drove out of the palace, he doing his best to keep her happy, and she quite obviously dreadfully shy.

At the Abbey the cheering was terrific. Princess Mary stepped out of the carriage in the most magnificent wedding dress and, as she entered the church, she dropped her bouquet, which her father picked up and handed back to her with a smile, whispering something (probably "Up socks!").

It was a radiant wedding as was any ceremony that Queen Mary arranged, for she was very clever at this sort of thing.

She was enchanted by the success of it and said: "In future we must have all the royal weddings here. It is the ideal background. Why didn't I think of it before?"

The Princess had gone off on her honeymoon – first to Shropshire, then to Florence – with what looked to be all London churning around her carriage, and the most powerful cheering that we had ever heard! Even if some people said that Lord Lascelles was too old for her, she seemed to be happy enough, and now everyone was prepared for the Prince of Wales

A family group: *back row*: the Prince of Wales (later George V); the Princess of Wales (later Queen Mary) holding Prince John (died aged 19); *front row*: Princess Mary (later the Princess Royal); Prince George (later Duke of Kent); Prince Edward (later Prince of Wales and Edward VIII); Prince Albert (later Duke of York and George VI); *seated*: Prince Henry (later Duke of Gloucester). Taken at Abergeldie in 1906

The Prince and Princess of Wales at Mar Lodge, Balmoral, in 1908

to marry next. It was high time that he met the princess of his dreams, so people said.

Privately the Queen felt unhappy about him. He had never been easy to manage, and now he was turning out to be most obstinate. She knew that he was having romantic affairs, but she hoped that eventually he would get sick of them and settle down, but her hopes were not fulfilled. David was in India at the time of his sister's wedding, of which he did not approve.

As people scooped up confetti in The Mall as souvenirs they said: "The Prince of Wales will be the next one of course," and that was just where they were wrong.

The Queen was worried because, growing older, there were moments when she wanted help with her unending engagements, and now could not rely entirely on her married daughter. But where David was perverse, her youngest surviving son, Prince George, was as easy-going as he was the best-looking of the Royal Family, and she had the feeling that he would marry somebody equally charming. He was the one who never failed her, so – with a sigh – she supposed that she would have to bide her time and that the Prince of Wales would eventually marry when *he* wished it, and not before.

Once, in a sad moment, when Princess Mary was in Yorkshire and perhaps her mother felt lonely, the Queen said, rather sadly, to a lady-in-waiting: "I do so miss the Princess. They say your son's your son till he gets him a wife, but your daughter's your daughter all her life. Somehow with Mary in Yorkshire it doesn't seem like that."

She was more disturbed than anything else about the King's health; he would not admit it, but he was frail and he had upsetting arguments with the heir to the throne. The war had decimated the royal families of Europe, and there were not the number of princesses from which the future Edward VIII could choose.

Privately the Queen fretted. She was one of those people who provides for the future and plans it so far as is possible. She had the feeling that life was not moving happily as it should do.

In the early spring of 1923 there came real joy into her life which was to ensure a long period of happiness. Prince Albert, the young Duke of York, who was rather a quiet young man with a stammer, and entirely different from his elder brother, made news.

(Mrs Bill had always said, "Now he is the good boy of the family. You can always trust him. He will do the right thing, and never any bother about doing it. He sticks to the rules.")

It was in the January of 1923 that he went, as he had often done before, to spend a week-end at St Paul's Waldenbury in Hertfordshire, seat of the Scottish Earl of Strathmore and Kinghorne, where he was always very happy. He had known them almost all his life: the Bowes-Lyon family home at Glamis Castle was not far from Balmoral.

It was surprisingly mild weather for the time of year, warm with a whisper of spring, so it seemed, and he went there this time presumably to shoot with the sons of the house. It was to prove an eventful week-end.

After luncheon on the Sunday, Bertie – the Royal Family's name for him – and the Lady Elizabeth Bowes-Lyon, who was the youngest daughter of Lord Strathmore's very large family, went for a walk in the woods. There is something wonderful about the first whisper of spring, even if it is still winter. They walked with the bare trees on either side of them, but the sun lit them with the first warmth of a new year.

They had met first at children's parties, and she was one of those few people with whom he was not shy. His stammer made him reluctant to meet people, as was only natural, but he and she, brought up together, could help each other. On that day, in the romantic wood, he asked her to marry him. She said Yes.

It was a love match, of course.

Bertie telephoned the family when they got back home and the Queen could hardly believe it. She felt such jubilation. If she had been suspicious that this might come, she certainly did not show it, and she was positively delighted. It had come so suddenly; she had never thought that Bertie would do so well.

"Just the right bride for him," she said, with motherly satisfaction.

It was the happiest thing that had happened at the palace for some time, and the King felt the same way. They thrilled with joy over the announcement. The charming girl was just the right bride for Bertie, and such a charming personality. The newspapers overflowed with exuberance, never had an engagement been better received, and nobody could have been more delighted than Queen Mary.

If the future bride was nervous, there was no need, and when the wedding came on 26th April of that year London completely lost its head! I have never seen it so joyous.

Elizabeth entered Westminster Abbey looking so tiny, almost like a little doll, and there was a slight hitch for somebody's clock had been wrong, which was most unusual for the Royal Family who lived by the clock. They had to wait a few moments. During the pause the bride slipped her bouquet on to the tomb of The Unknown Warrior.

There were bigger crowds than I had ever seen before. The reception, held at Buckingham Palace, was almost rowdy, for the sons of the house were there to enjoy the occasion, and enjoy it they did! The King was roaring with laughter as he flung confetti after the bride and bridegroom, and the Queen said it was one of the happiest days of her life. She knew they would be happy, for Elizabeth was such a darling, and obviously it *was* a real love match, and this was the reason why the country went so mad about it. Being in love was the best possible reason for getting married, and it does not always come to royals.

Nobody knew at that particular time that the poor little bride was sickening for whooping cough, and she took this on her honeymoon with her, which was not so good, poor girl! What an acquisition to the family she was!

Queen Alexandra died after a heart attack, though she had been ill at Sandringham for some time. It was towards the end of 1925, and there was an impressive funeral service, which Queen Mary attended with her husband. The Queen was deeply touched by it, for she had always liked her mother-in-law, though she doubted if Queen Alexandra ever heard much that she said. That night she wrote in her diary, rather sadly:

> Now darling Mamma lies with dear Eddy.

This must have been the first time for years that she had referred to her first fiancé, whom she had watched die, a tragedy she would never forget.

Now Sandringham was free again! "We shall be going home," she wrote to a friend, "and this is something I have always longed to do. I hope it hasn't changed too much, but doubt it. Sandringham is always home to us."

The death of the King's mother plunged them into mourning, but in the spring of 1926 there was the joy of a baby soon to come to the Duke and Duchess of York. Queen Mary knitted busily for it. As yet the young Yorks had not found a permanent home for themselves which was difficult. They had first lived at White Lodge – Queen Mary's old home and birthplace of her eldest son – but the arrangement was that this baby would be born at the Strathmore's London house in Bruton Street, Mayfair.

The Queen had been 'house-hunting' for them. She was very good at this, and her eldest son once said that "if the Crown gave mother up, she would have to start as a land agent, and sell houses, for she knew all about the job!" She had found a home for them at 145 Piccadilly; ultimately they moved in and for many years were to be very happy there.

The arrival of the royal baby never took the headlines for, although she was a most important child (the Prince of Wales showing no sign of marrying), there were other pieces of news that seemed to be more urgent.

The future Queen Elizabeth II had arrived in the midst of the General Strike, at a time when we were not used to strikes, as we are today. The whole of England was so surprised by it that it did not know if it was standing on its head or its feet. Hyde Park had changed completely, and seemed to be one enormous barracks. Once could not count the number of tents in it.

Everybody was extremely worried about the strike, getting food in (in case it ran out), and that sort of thing, so that the birth of a future Queen of England was recorded under modest headlines. To the editors of the day nothing was more urgent than the strike news.

The King and Queen were called about three o'clock in the early morning, as they had asked to be notified at any hour. The little duchess (as we all knew her) had given birth to a princess at 2.40 a.m. on 21st April.

"That is just what we wanted," said her glad grandmother, for she had had only one daughter herself, and would have loved to have had more.

There was no reason to want a grandson, for in time the Prince of Wales would be sure to marry. The King and Queen rose earlier than usual that morning, and immediately after breakfast drove to the mansion in Bruton Street (since demolished). It was reported that she was much more like her father than her mother; and, of course, at this particular moment, few people even dreamt that she would ever reign, although next day the *Daily Mail* pointed out: "The baby who was the chief topic of conversation throughout the Kingdom yesterday could conceivably become Queen of England."

When suitable time had elapsed, and England had recovered somewhat from that dreadful strike, the new baby was christened at Buckingham Palace on 29th May. She wore the Honiton lace robe, now treated more carefully for it was getting rather frail and needed guarding. She received the names of Elizabeth Alexandra Mary, a very abbreviated set of names, so it seemed. And now, for the first time the name Victoria had faded away.

The reports said that the baby was "very good", although, as Queen Mary recorded: "Of course poor baby cried."

This extremely happy marriage of her second son compensated poor Queen Mary for some of her anxiety about the Prince of Wales, who made miracle tours on behalf of the King (carrying them out magnificently), but was no nearer meeting a Princess of Wales, and this was what everybody was talking about.

"When will the Prince of Wales marry?" everybody was asking, now more and more urgently. It seemed to be rather a long delay.

It worried the Queen enormously, and the King had talked with David and told him that marriage was his duty. His mother tried to think that perhaps he wanted a fling before he settled down, and she was worried about his riding and hunting, and having some bad falls, one a really bad one which made the King step in and stop it happening again.

The Prince usually agreed with what his parents said, and yet never met the right girl, and did nothing about it. He certainly did not dislike women, he had many nice girl friends, she knew, but not one of them seemed nice enough for him to want to settle down with.

Undoubtedly the Queen tried to guide him, but, as he grew older, he became ever more difficult to advise – that acute obstinacy which Mrs Bill had complained about in him as a boy, and had said that he should "be got out of it before he harmed himself with it".

And these old nannies *know*!

David's future again became a matter of public comment when the marriage of the young Duke of Kent suddenly came into the headlines in 1934. David's youngest brother went abroad for his bride and became engaged while everyone was summer-holidaying. He had fallen deeply in love with one of the most beautiful princesses in Europe, if not quite *the* most beautiful, and also the best dressed. She was the lovely Princess Marina of Greece.

When she heard the good news the Queen was enchanted. She rose and fell on her toes, as usual, when she discussed it. The news came when the King and Queen were staying at Balmoral.

"They must come up here and visit us at once," said the Queen.

Princess Marina, with her gift of good dressing, entirely changed our rather dowdy fashions here. Queen Mary had always adhered to the same type of clothes, which was a pity. She had superb good taste in arranging a room, or planning a garden, but when it came to dress, save on the very big occasions, the styles she selected did not suit her, although they suited the King. She followed the same mode all the time, unfortunately.

The little Duchess of York had brought good taste into the royal circle. We copied her tiny hats, and the way that she always wore a flower in her coat, and her charmingly pretty things. Princess Mary dressed rather like her mother.

But Princess Marina was the first princess of that generation who loved good dressing, and she arrived in England looking most attractive. She chose plain, well-cut clothes, and within a week every one of us was trying to copy her.

Prince George and his fiancée went straight up to Balmoral, and the Queen was enchanted by her radiantly beautiful new daughter-in-law-to-be. We all realized that the engagement would be fairly brief, for short engagements had become the rule in the Royal Family. It had been Queen Victoria who had insisted on that, and these days nobody was engaged very long. It would be another Westminster Abbey wedding, and, with the bride's good taste as a guide, possibly the loveliest of them all.

At this time the Queen had become extremely worried about the King's health, which had been declining since a nearly fatal illness in 1928, though not for the world would she have admitted this. He was not very willing to take advice, and he refused to have the general overhaul which she wanted for him. He also was elated by the prospect of a royal wedding in November.

There would be two best men, as is usual with a royal bridegroom – the Prince of Wales and his brother Henry, the Duke of Gloucester, attending him.

On the morning of the wedding there was a dense fog; you could hardly see your hand in front of your face, a real 'pea-souper'. As the hour of the marriage came nearer the fog did not lift, but this did not deter huge London crowds from gathering along the route. The whole of the ceremony was to be broadcast – the first time that it had happened at a royal wedding; those waiting in the streets would hear it also, for there were microphones all along the route, a tremendous advance, we all felt.

In places the fog was so thick that we heard only the muted sounds of car wheels, and saw almost nothing. When the car with the bride in it arrived, the brilliance of diamonds shimmered through the murk. She was the first royal bride to wear a tiara.

Queen Mary had suggested it. "A lovely change," she said. "How lovely it is! Aren't we lucky to have such a radiant bride in the family?"

The King got a tremendous reception when he entered the Abbey, but the Queen watched him carefully. She knew that he had never really recovered from the horse rolling on him in the war, though she never said anything: he could be touchy if people suggested that he was not well.

She said: "If I keep mentioning it, it is nagging, and that is vile! I just hope that he will be careful; he always does far too much, of course."

The Kents lived in London for a while and once again it was the Queen who found them a house, this time in Belgravia. It was there that their first baby was born on 9th October 1935. An enormous crowd was there that night, and a great number of reporters. I remember that about nine o'clock a large black cat walked up the step and settled itself down there. Everyone said it was a good omen, and brought them luck. The baby was a boy.

He was christened later at Buckingham Palace, wearing *the* christening robe, and given the names of Edward George Nicholas Paul Patrick. The Queen loved being a grandmother again, but Prince Edward's birth was overshadowed by fresh anxiety about the King's health, and also by reports that the Prince of Wales and his father were not seeing eye-to-eye.

David had grown more difficult still, while the King was so unwell that several times the Queen had to take his place at some public function.

Mercifully she herself retained marvellous good health almost to the end of her life, although rarely did any woman suffer more shocks, or go through more difficult times, than she did.

"I am fortunate to be so strong," she told people. But she was a wise woman who seldom took risks. "One only has one life to live," she once said, "and if my feet don't give out I shall live to a ripe old age."

But being royal *is* hard on the feet!

All this time she was hoping that one day her eldest son would "spring a surprise on us", and said that she would be the person most delighted about it. Alas, the surprise that he *did* eventually spring was not quite as she had anticipated.

The old days of Queen Victoria had disappeared into the past. She had arranged her family's marriages, and she would, so Queen Mary felt, somehow have controlled this difficult son of hers. It seemed all wrong that he should remain in the bachelor state, for he was a marvellous ambassador for Britain, he had been very brave in the First World War, and she admired much that he did. But, for some reason or other, and she could not discover why, he would *not* conform to the usual rules of the marriage of the heir to the crown. All his brothers were now happily married – Henry, Duke of Gloucester, had married the seventh Duke of Buccleuch's daughter Alice in November, 1935.

"Perhaps it will happen suddenly," said the Queen one day to a very old friend at Sandringham. "He will meet the right girl and that will be that. It would be very wonderful if he did."

The Kents had a second baby coming in the winter of 1936, for that year the Duchess could not go down to Sandringham with the Royal Family, as her new baby would arrive somewhere about that date. A princess was born on Christmas morning, and oh, how very very welcome she was!

The reports were that she was strikingly like her lovely mother, and she was baptized in the same gown and given the names of Alexandra Helen Elizabeth Olga Christabel. The Queen was in touch with her daughter-in-law from Sandringham on that very day. She spoke to her before the light dimmed, and as the family Christmas tree blazed in full glory.

"I'm so glad that the baby is a girl," she said; "we have never had enough girls in this family."

The Queen was extremely happy with her grandchildren, and was said to spoil them far more than she had ever spoilt her own children.

"Ever so fond of them all, she was," said Mrs Bill; "would have done anything for them at any time."

The doctors now warned the Queen that her husband would not last very long. It was difficult to induce him to take proper care of himself, and the one thing she insisted on was that he must never be made to do anything he did not wish to do.

"I have seen so many invalids simply pestered to death," she said, "and that is so unfair. Whilst one lives, one should live in peace."

He was particularly happy with the little Princess Elizabeth, whom he adored, and who had been a regular visitor to her grandfather ever since the King's first almost fatal illness in 1928, when during his convalescence at Bognor Regis she often rode with him in his bath-chair.

Now, as Christmas of 1935 approached, the Queen realized that his life was slowly veering towards its end. The world, of course, did not know what a very sick man he was.

7

Widowhood

The doctors did not think that the King was well enough to go down to Sandringham that Christmas.

But she persisted.

"It means such a lot to him," she said, for she knew that he would hate to miss it, and not going might make him worse.

So he did go down to "dear old Sandringham".

"I need the strong Norfolk air," he said, "and that is my home, my real home."

It had always been the way that he had looked at it.

He brightened considerably as they approached Liverpool Street station, with the royal train waiting for them, and the officials in a line ready to receive them. The station was garlanded for him, and the Queen knew that the sight of it would help him. He felt better already, he said, as he walked to the waiting train.

The King flagged somewhat on the journey, and she watched him closely all the time. "He must *not* overtire himself," she told others, "that is the important thing. He must not get too tired."

When the train pulled into Wolferton station near Sandringham, there was the station-master, whom they knew so well, in his best uniform, with holly in his cap. The King said how glad he was to be 'home' again, and, as he walked to the waiting car, he actually laughed.

Here they were; the Squire and his wife, not King and Queen, and they were coming home for Christmas.

"It's good to be back," they said.

She had the feeling that Sandringham loved them and would

be kind to them. Coming home could only do the King good. He had a rest but came down for dinner that first night, because the carol party would be around later and they would be asked inside to sing there to him. The evening went off remarkably well, and she told herself that she had been right to ignore the doctors' doubts.

He went to bed early on her advice, but he was one of those men who did not take kindly to being fussed, and he found it very difficult to be treated as an invalid.

"I'm not ill," he protested. "I get tired, but that's because I'm older. These doctors make such a fuss. Send for the doctor and then you *will* be ill."

Under it all there lay this other worry, the family concern which the King called, "This Mrs Simpson business".

The Prince of Wales had a perfect right to choose his own friends, but he was getting himself talked about. His friendship with the Simpsons worried the family.

The Queen herself had spoken to her son about the danger of getting gossip going. The country looked to him to marry the right girl when the time came. But David's angle was that it is in no way unusual for a family to dislike their son's friends. He was of another generation. Everything had changed with the World War; surely his parents realized this?

The Queen remembered when she had been a girl and her mother had worried about her brothers' friends at times. It happened with sons. Possibly this was what befalls most mothers, but when you are the Queen and your son is the future King, then things are a great deal more difficult.

Mrs Wallis Simpson was presented at Court, but somehow Queen Mary could not remember her. Possibly she did become aware of the fact that her eldest son was drifting further and further away. But he is *my* son, she told herself.

Whatever happened he would always be her son and she would do everything in her power to help him. But now, down at Sandringham for Christmas, she would put all worries away and concentrate on her husband's well-being.

Sandringham always inspired them. Good seasonable weather came with the New Year and gave the King a chance to improve. But the Queen had a premonition; she remembered the tragedy of Sandringham when Prince Albert Victor had died here; she would never forget her mother-in-law's grief and her own despair!

"Not again!" she told herself with horror. "I could not bear that again."

The first weeks went well, coming home had given the King new spirit, he was able to go out, and he met people whom he liked to see.

Then he caught a chill. The newspapers mentioned it, and that was the first time we knew something was really wrong. The guests were leaving. The Queen had known for months that this *could* happen, and fairly suddenly. She was very brave, but she must have known that there was very little hope.

The two little Princesses – Elizabeth and Margaret Rose (born at Glamis Castle in 1930) – left for London with Mrs Knight, their nurse, and that was another sign that worried the country. George V had been part of our lives, and we could not bear to think of his going. At Liverpool Street station Princess Elizabeth eluded Mrs Knight, for she had caught sight of the King's specialist, waiting also for his train. She made a dash for him and begged him to "make Grandpa better".

He tried to be reassuring.

The Queen spent all her time with the invalid. The house seemed to be very quiet with no guests there, but it was that quiet which precedes the end. They had been together for so many years, and possibly meant more to each other than most of our kings and queens. Her second son begged her to rest, but she said that she could not rest until the King was better; yet, even as she said it, she must have known, deep down in her heart, that he would never be better again.

It had been the ordinary report on the King's health, until the late afternoon of a bleak day in January when it changed to these words, which Queen Mary herself had asked them to use:

"The King's life is passing peacefully to its close".

No more! Just the truth, and it was a truth that must have hurt her most terribly.

Nothing more could be done, and it was almost midnight on the 20th when the end came. Then, with complete calmness, she rose and curtseyed to her eldest son, who had in that moment become Edward VIII. Was it then that she became really afraid for him, and did she ask herself questions about the future? I doubt it. She would believe that, in assuming the crown, he knew he would have to change his life, for the King *is* the king.

She wrote in her diary:

> At 5 to 12, my darling husband passed peacefully away. My children were angelic to me.

Later she wrote these further lines, which show how truly and how deeply affected she was:

> The sunset of his death ringed the whole world's sky.

She knew that everything would change and we would enter a new age. She was prepared for this, but in that hour she could never have guessed how much she would be tested. For the moment the new King was goodness itself to her. She hoped that he would change his outlook, and his tenderness encouraged her greatly.

King Edward had to fly back to London next morning, which he did in his own 'plane. Her other sons were with her, and her daughters-in-law, also. Perhaps, she told herself, this will bring everything right again? Perhaps now that he is King, David will understand? She believed that.

But three days later the papers published a picture of the new king at St James's Palace, watching his proclamation. And standing with him was Mrs Simpson.

8

The Eleven-Month King

The Queen had known for many years now, and so had Mrs Bill, that, although she could trust implicitly all her children, the one who might err was the one who mattered the most to England. For the moment the news was "The King is dead, long live the King", and she was wrestling with her own deep distress and at the same time trying to prepare herself to face the ordeal of a state funeral, which asks far too much of everyone in the royal circle. I am sure at this time she still had faith in her eldest son, and truly believed that he would do well. He had had a long, intensive training for the throne. But she was not sure about his present background.

Without her knowing it she had been given a sleeping draught which helped her recover her poise after the King's death. Mercifully she had always been a very strong woman, and possibly she could face trials that would have destroyed others.

"I shall be all right," she told her children. "You must not worry for me, because I knew a long time ago that this would come. *I shall be all right*."

That afternoon the King's coffin was closed for ever, and when the dusk came (it was a frosty night) he was carried across the park, to be laid in the little Sandringham church. His piper went with him, and the almost eerie sound of the pipes wailed out into the darkness of the night. The Queen followed him. Nothing would have made her stay away. Apparently she was calm, for she had always been a singularly brave woman, and whatever happened, she would do her duty to the end. They went into that lovely little church with its silver chancel, where the King would rest until he was taken to Windsor for burial.

Her doctors had tried to stop her from going, but quietly, and with complete detachment, she said: "Not only was he my husband, he was also my King!"

There had been a keen wind blowing when she walked out of Sandringham House behind her husband's coffin into the darkness of the park. She said to one of her ladies that the air smelt of snow, what she always called "the Sandringham scent". She had suffered far too much already, and it seems that she was one of those people particularly selected for sorrow, although she was certainly not a 'tragic queen' like Mary, Queen of Scots or Marie Antoinette. She did not know that the future would be even more 'unlucky'. She believed that her first-born would do what he had been trained to do and would never betray the crown.

To a woman who had never for a single moment failed in what she considered to be her duty, the ultimate end of that affair must have been the most appalling blow of all. But on that dark January evening she had no inkling of this.

At the lych-gate of the little country church they were met by the Sandringham rector, and the guardsmen carried the coffin into the church which George V had always loved. It was set down before the altar, with the men from the estate to keep guard over him, until the hour came for his body to be taken to London for the lying-in-state. The Queen wrote of it quite composedly:

> We had a very comforting short service, and the church was full of our own kind people. Such a sad day! It is curious my having been present in this house at the death of the two brothers, Eddy and George.

Possibly this was the first time that she had referred in writing to Prince Albert Victor for years. She had been young when he had died, and now she was old. But, as she wrote to a friend, nothing lessens the sadness of death or relieves the pain.

It seemed strange that, at this time, she should have

remembered her first love, for there were so very, very few moments in her life when she ever mentioned him. You might almost have thought that he had never been, but that was not so. She was always wounded by the memory. Queen Mary was a woman who never forgot.

When Edward VII had died there had been quite a long interval between his death and the subsequent interment at Windsor. This had worried her.

"It took far too long and it is a dreadful strain that should not be," she had said.

She asked that this should not be repeated now.

On 23rd January the body of the King was taken on a gun carriage and brought through the rhododendron-edged lanes of Norfolk on the start of his journey. The train awaited him at Wolferton station. The station-master who knew him so well was waiting, too. It was one of those radiant and beautiful days that come to that part of the world at this time, a day of sunshine which conveys the impression that spring is not far behind, much like that January long ago when the Duke of York had proposed to Elizabeth Bowes-Lyon.

The Queen said to her daughter, "I am glad that the sun is shining, for that always helps."

She tried to keep a firm grip on herself, for she must not break down. She had refused to take something that the doctor thought would help her, determined to rely solely upon her own resources. At the same time she felt intensely miserable and alone.

When the cortège arrived at Liverpool Street station, another gun-carriage awaited them. Queen Mary suddenly thought of the way that she and the King had started on this Christmas holiday journey together, how happy she had been thinking that he felt better, and that the Norfolk air would give him new life. She had the greatest faith in Norfolk. Now it was the funeral, with the Imperial Crown standing on the King's coffin, guarded by soldiers.

The Queen Mother managed to maintain her regal calm; she was entirely tearless. She had never been what her family in her youth would have called a 'cry-baby'; brought up with only brothers, she rather scorned weeping. Dry-eyed she stepped into her coach, Princess Mary (the Princess Royal) with her, and she set forth stoically on the slow, slow procession to Westminster Hall at the Houses of Parliament.

The cortège had got as far as Charing Cross station when something went wrong and, although she said nothing, it upset the poor Queen very much indeed when she heard about it. She had never been a very superstitious woman, yet she could not help but feel that it was not a good omen.

The crown was on the coffin. I was at Charing Cross and saw it happen absolutely in front of me; suddenly it looked as if the crown were falling! I thought that I was dreaming.

A soldier marching immediately behind the coffin saw it before I did, put out his hand and caught something. He acted amazingly quickly; he was a company sergeant-major. With a deft move he righted the crown and slipped something into his pocket: it was the Maltese Cross which had fallen from the Imperial Crown into the gutter.

Already there had been sufficient gossip about the new King watching his own proclamation at St James's Palace with Mrs Simpson at his side. That worried us all.

The Queen could not have seen what happened at the procession, for she and the Princess Royal were in the carriage too far back behind them to see it. But, of course, she read about it in the papers and at this highly emotional moment in her life it is understandable that she was grieved. The new King saw the incident. He was walking just behind the guardsman and he wrote in his diary:

> It was such a strange thing to happen, and, although I am not superstitious, I wondered if it was a bad omen.

It was, of course, a very bad omen.

The Queen told one of her ladies that she had been a little superstitious, which she felt to be rather silly of her. Apparently she had been to a soothsayer as a girl, before her engagement to Prince Eddy, and had been told: "You will be a Queen, but not the Queen of your first love." She had never forgotten this, and although she tried to dismiss such things as being "rather silly", she could not help but remember this one.

I suppose most of us thought that the obvious 'tottering of the crown' of England on the coffin of King George V was a very bad sign, especially as we knew Mrs Simpson was already on the scene. Fate proved us to be right.

The Queen went to Westminster with David and then straight to Buckingham Palace. "I am so thankful to be back," she told her ladies.

Some photographs of the King with Mrs Simpson watching his proclamation appeared in every newspaper. The Queen would have seen them, of course, and must have formed her own conclusions. But at this time she had the sympathy and comfort that her second son and his charming family could offer her, and she needed it all.

She would probably have convinced herself that the 'tottering crown' was nothing, did not mean a thing. But if she had hoped that what was known as 'the Simpson affair' would have come to an end when he became king, she was wrong.

The Queen was worried that her son had been so foolish as to let the photograph be taken; he and Mrs Simpson should have been prepared for it, as royalty learns to be. Then she thought that perhaps she was old-fashioned (the excuse that people growing older always make for themselves), for the world had changed enormously, and frankly some of the things that happened she just could not understand.

"He's not getting his own way with me," Mrs Bill had said, and she had stuck to that one. But she was more fortunate than some of those with whom he came into contact in later years.

During the war the Queen and he had come close together. His handsome looks drew from her the proud comment that it was "quite a pleasure to look at him". She had been very proud of his magnificent tours, and all that he had done for the country, which adored him.

But what he was doing now was *wrong*!

The late King had always said: "David will be a good king if he is not too pig-headed about it, but he always wants his own way, and even a king cannot get it every time. He's got to learn that one."

The days of the lying-in-state were horrible for her, but she never shed a tear in public, though she must have wept bitterly behind the scenes, especially over that wretched photograph. Her great comfort was her young family, especially the grandchildren. The two York princesses in particular came and went continually and, as she once said, "When you are really sad, children can be such a big help."

She was thankful when the King's burial at Windsor was done, and then she could take things more easily, the strain behind her. She would, of course, move into Marlborough House, her old home and one on which she had lavished so much care and planning. She had alterations made, and the workmen on the job were surprised by the intelligent questions she asked.

Her ideas were still surprisingly good, and she was insistent that things must be done *her* way.

Although the new monarch was very busy, he was very good in visiting her and seeing to her needs, but of course the agony of being left widowed does not end with the husband's death. There were innumerable papers to be gone through, and some of these brought back hurtful memories. Until now she had not realized how much such memories *could* hurt. She told herself that she must look forward, not back. The King came to her for help in the planning of the coronation, for she had the most retentive memory and could recall details of the two previous coronations, and this helped. But all the time the Queen had a feeling that the future was in a haze. She told the Duchess of York that it never did to look too far ahead; live the day for itself – that was the true answer to life. This sounded very unlike her, but her life had changed and so had she.

In the July the period of mourning ended, for the new King made it shorter than it had ever been before. His argument was that it did no good, and was bad for the country, and this was possibly true.

He also held two afternoon presentations at Buckingham Palace for the large number of debutantes waiting to be received by the new Sovereign. There had been the hold-up whilst the Court was in mourning, for whilst they wore black nothing of this sort could happen. He made a complete change, having discussed the possibilities with his mother. How would it be to have an afternoon Court, held in the gardens of the palace, which were very lovely indeed?

The Queen rose and fell on her toes with enthusiasm.

"That is quite a wonderful idea," she said; "why have we never thought of it before? An afternoon Court in the gardens, tea in a big tent, quite a new background."

However, it was one of those unfortunate English summer days when the weather does not play fair. Her first inquiry on the morning was: "Is the weather all right?" and then it seemed to augur a real heatwave day. Everyone was feeling thrilled by the thought of this unique Court when, about midday, a nasty little cloud appeared from nowhere, rapidly spreading across the sky. It had been the most brilliant morning, too good perhaps, and nobody had been prepared for the downpour which followed.

The debs gathered in glorious sunshine, against a most remarkable setting. Some of them had been presented when the cloud appeared, and the sun vanished, so that the last few in the queue were very apprehensive, for it threatened to pour at any moment, and so it did!

"You can never really trust the English weather," the Queen

said rather sadly; she already knew that this was an experiment which would never be repeated.

She herself went to see the Trooping the Colour ceremony on Horse Guards Parade on 16th July. The King presented new colours to six Guards battalions, and when returning from the ceremony there was a nasty scene. The Queen herself, back at the palace to greet her son, was horrified when she was told what had happened. The King had been riding home along Constitution Hill, with the Duke of York just behind him, when a man, pushing himself forward through the crowd, waved a revolver at the King's horse. The Duke of York saw this starting to happen, just a moment before the King himself realized it, and he pressed forward, putting himself and his own horse between the man and his Sovereign. It was a very brave action to take, and I thought that the newspapers might have made a good deal more of it.

As it happened the would-be assassin – an Irishman named McMahon – tossed the loaded gun over the heads of the crowd to draw attention to his grievances.

It was one of those things that had frequently happened to Queen Victoria, they all knew, and one cannot guard against the risk, but in that day and generation it should not have happened, and it surprised the world.

The Queen Mother was deeply shocked for she thought she saw more behind it. She knew by now that a great deal of gossip was going on about the King and Mrs Simpson, and she felt him most unwise to continue the affair. The lady had had two husbands already; the first she had divorced to marry the second, and now there were rumours that the same thing was going to happen with the second. It would be quite frightful if she was doing this with the idea of marrying the King, for as his mother thought she knew, that could never be!

She felt suddenly alone. It was the Duke of York who comforted her.

"He would never do anything so silly," he said.

But once David got an idea into his head he stuck to it, even when he himself must have known that some of his ideas were silly, and his mother realized this.

The name 'Mrs Simpson' was on everybody's lips. ("And there is absolutely nothing that I can do about it," she told her second son.) She argued with herself that surely the hour would come when her son appreciated that he could not do this sort of thing, and that ultimately he and Mrs Simpson must part.

Outwardly she appeared tranquil, preserving the royal manner always. She was preparing to retire to her own house as the Queen Mother. She had to divest herself of the crown jewels, which she handed back to the new King. She consulted him about everything she did. Outwardly one would have thought that there was nothing wrong between them, but inwardly one knew that everything was wrong.

Foreign newspapers discussed the affair. Surely, if he read them, the King would realize that if he married the lady he could not remain on the throne? What ought I to *do*? she asked herself.

On 30th July she finally left Buckingham Palace and drove down to Sandringham. She had never been too fond of the palace, which Victoria until her widowhood had adored, and none of her heirs were keen about it, of course – too big, too demanding, and too draughty! She went home to Norfolk for a breath of fresh air.

It would be pleasant for, as she had once said, "You can never make a big palace your home, for the two things simply do not go together, and it is always first of all a palace, and only secondly a home."

It was good to be back at Sandringham, to walk about the gardens and visit old friends, but all the time she felt tormented by the what-is-David-going-to-do? question.

She was now deeply concerned as they came nearer to the year of the coronation, with everything that it meant. She would go back to Marlborough House, which she had changed considerably, and out of her own purse ("That is only honest," she said, "the country should not pay because I want things changed," and she gave that infectiously merry laugh of hers!).

More and more she resented David's affair with a divorcee, which she had so devoutedly hoped would have ended with George V's death. This affair was lasting far too long!

Once she said to her daughter, "I suppose it had to happen. David was always stubborn. But, of course, the break has got to come. Then what will he do?"

The Princess Royal, who knew David better than most, thought that he would give up the crown rather than the woman. Her bluntness appalled the Queen Mother, the more so because she recognized that there was an element of truth behind it.

"But how could he do that? Bertie's stammer would make it hopelessly difficult for him to reign. David would never push that on to him, surely?"

The Princess Royal was not so sure, because, as she said, men in love do very funny things, and she had read some of the French papers (which printed all the news about it that they could get) and very staggering it was to her..He was not getting over it as they had hoped and as he had got over his earlier affairs. He had had passing crazes.

"I believe 'crushes' is the modern name for them," the Queen said rather sadly. But those 'crushes' had always petered out after a while.

That summer the King went for a holiday cruise in the Mediterranean aboard the chartered yacht *Nahlin*, and from the moment that he set foot on deck he became the news story of the year, because he took with him, among others, the 'married lady from Baltimore'. The Queen Mother was utterly dismayed. Pictures were published of him walking hand in hand on foreign shores with Mrs Simpson out shopping, and enjoying life. Quite clearly they were lovers!

The Queen Mother turned to her daughter, who adored him

and understood him. "Where, and how, does this end?" she demanded.

Now she was half afraid to open a foreign paper lest she see still something more about him. The pair were quite obviously in love, and she sympathized with this, but she, knowing him, realized that argument would make it worse. Was he going to push the crown overboard?

"He *is* the King," she told her daughter. And how demeaning it was to have Europe chattering, for this was news in quite a big way.

"Yes, but he ... he cares for her," the Princess Royal said.

"You ... you think that it will end?" the Queen Mother asked with some hesitation, for inwardly she did not think this.

Princess Mary did not think that it would end either, for she knew the grim determination of her favourite brother, and Mrs Bill warning him, "You can't do that and stay happy", which was a warning that he ought to recall now.

That summer holiday with the attendant publicity was a step in the wrong direction, and undoubtedly his mother knew it. The couple never tried to conceal their affection for each other from their friends and intimates.

David wrote to his mother, but told her nothing, and it was all too difficult for her, for she was not too well, not having recovered from the strain of her husband's illness and death. Her daughter consoled her – though without much conviction – by expressing the belief that the trouble would pass; she ought to remember, she told her mother, how good David was at changing his mind (which was true), and this helped her a little.

"Surely he cannot think that he can marry the lady and be happy?" she asked, and then, "The date for the coronation is already fixed. This affair ought to stop before he is crowned. It's all wrong."

The thought of demeaning the crown of England haunted her. Her daughter had seldom seen her cry before, but she did now. Her son wrote from the *Nahlin* to say where they were going, and what fun it all was. He felt like a new man! He did not mention Mrs Simpson, but told her that when he returned he was going to Balmoral, as usual, for a fortnight with a really lively house party of the sort she could never have entertained there. She could have wept when she read the letter. Obviously he was most desperately in love and, with the gay rapture of all lovers, believed that it would all come out right in the end and that it was no business of anyone else's. Indeed, throughout this sad period the King kept the Royal Family at a distance, especially the Heir Presumptive, the Duke of York.

Mrs Simpson's divorce went through at Ipswich, of all places, with little or no publicity at home, extremely quietly, for they had managed to hide it from the Press until the last minute. There would be the long period of waiting before the decree *nisi* became absolute, and surely that would bring the King to reason, his mother thought. She received lots of letters from her subjects, begging her "to do something about it", but what could she do? The letters received a polite acknowledgement. No more.

"I'm growing older," she told one of her ladies. "Things worry me much more, and I do get quite tired."

In October she moved into Marlborough House for good. And I hope it is for ever, she said, for she had moved too many times in her life to want to continue the process. She lunched with the King at the palace, a friendly, happy lunch with no mention of the divorce, or of the fact that the lady was in London and that he saw her. In fact he was at his best, reassuring her so that she half wondered if he was turning over a new leaf and meant to cast off his American love, as he had cast off others before Mrs Simpson. It was almost too much to hope, she told herself.

They talked of coronation plans, now the first thoughts in all minds, and she gave him helpful details of her own experiences.

He was very attentive to all this.

It seemed to be almost like the old days, and afterwards they drove down The Mall together to Marlborough House, where he had tea with her. It was the first tea against the old amiable family background, which she had now much improved, and she thought of it as being one of the happiest afternoons of her life. David can be such a dear boy, she told herself, and she had faith in him.

But when he had gone fresh batches of foreign newspapers reached her and harassed her. It was dreadful what they knew, or said they knew. There was that strange quirk in his nature; the mere fact that anyone was (what he called) "against him" would encourage him to fight on, like Don Quixote.

By the autumn of 1936 the Queen Mother's worst fears were realized, for the danger was increasing! It was now quite plain that he was *not* giving up Mrs Simpson whatever the crown asked of him. The lady came of good American stock, and had lived in Maryland. Both her earlier husbands, from what the newspapers said, had been nice men, and, of course, in the United States, divorce was an everyday affair. Nobody thought too much of it as they did in Britain.

Another who was suffering a great deal, too, was the Princess Royal. Her own marriage was not turning out well, though nothing was said about it but she had gone back to her mother for the time being. That first remarkable marriage in the Abbey of the new royal generation had not been the pathway to real happiness, it seemed.

"But I am so glad to have her home," the Queen said.

Her anxiety was that her son seemed to be getting himself a wife with two divorces behind her, and that the Established Church – of which he was the Head – would not tolerate it.

Princess Mary again reminded her that her brother had always been obdurate. She could not be quite sure of him, though she could not believe that he would let everyone down: Mrs Bill's training had been too good for that.

But this was the one time when poor Mrs Bill had not been entirely successful, though, as yet, they did not know it.

The Queen spoke to her second son about it, and he was even more worried than she was, for, if David abdicated, where could he be, handicapped as he was? The Queen was wondering what the Prime Minister, Mr Baldwin, would do, for he was the man who would have to take action at what he thought to be the right time.

"I do so pray that never happens," she said, rather miserably, for it would be a nightmare, and she told her daughter this.

The suspense deepened. Things could not go on like this for ever. The hour came when the Prime Minister visited the palace to see the King. His answer was naïve. Edward VIII intended to marry the lady of his choice the moment she was free to do so!

The Queen Mother, when she heard what had happened, wondered how poor Mr Baldwin had taken it. He was calm but dismayed. He told the King that the plans for the coronation were far advanced, and he could not marry a woman with two divorces behind her and be Head of the Church of England.

The King then suggested that his next brother should "take on for him".

It was a shocking interview for both of them, as the King was adamant. The Queen gathered that Mr Baldwin left the palace that night with cold horror in his heart, for he realized then that the bitter truth was that the King would have to abdicate. There was no other way out if he persisted like this.

The Queen Mother's pity went out to her second son, by far the nicer man, a shy boy who disliked crowds, who was diffident in company. He and his sweet little duchess would have to leave their happy home life at 145 Piccadilly and at The Royal Lodge near Windsor for the palace, and what could she do to help them, for she knew what the palace asked of people.

"It is unbearable," she told her daughter, who was appalled that this crisis had come and her brother was going through with his plans.

"I will see him, Mamma," she said – and she did, but already it was far too late.

In her heart the Queen Mother must have known that her second son would be the better king, but it was a most terrible position to be in, and she wept.

"To have this at the end of one's life is so awful," she said to her daughter.

At this time the little Duchess of York was ill with an influenza which had turned to pneumonia. This had been kept out of the Press. Slowly recovering, this constitutional crisis was not the 'tonic' that she wanted, for it was terrifying.

Her mother-in-law, weeping with her daughter, said: "Poor little Elizabeth! This is the most dreadful thing to happen to anyone, for the strain is so awful."

And if anybody knew what the strain felt like, she was the one!

She got in touch with her eldest son, thinking that he would stubbornly refuse to see her, but he was quite willing and ready to come to Marlborough House to visit her there. He was kind, and understanding, she felt, but that ruthless obstinacy of his held him back. She told him that he was betraying his country and his crown.

He retorted that his private life was his own. He was very much in love with the lady, and as far as he was concerned there was no other woman in the world for him. He reiterated that he intended to marry her the moment that she was free.

When he was young she had always said, "David is the obstinate one, and he must learn that he can't get his own way." This was the lesson that he never learnt.

"Though I did try," Mrs Bill told me, "he was his own worst enemy", and there she was right.

His mother remonstrated with him in that long argument of theirs. She told him that he was putting himself before his country; his reply was that he had the right to do what he chose. He was in love for the first time in his life (which was not exactly true, and she knew this, for she was a very far-seeing woman) and he had to follow the promptings of his heart.

She tried another ploy. "Bertie is not strong enough to fill the king's role," she said. "It would be terrible for him, you must know that!"

When he finally left, still determined to marry Mrs Simpson, she broke down and wept on her daughter's shoulder. Later she felt ashamed that she had done it, but this *was* her darkest hour. He meant to go through with it. There was no dissuading him. He was resolved to abdicate.

9

King George VI

The King left Buckingham Palace for his Fort Belvedere retreat near Windsor, for all of a sudden he was getting the response of the public to his behaviour, and they were extremely averse to the way that he was acting. Surely he could not abdicate like this, and just walk out of all our lives. Christmas was around the corner. The Queen Mother fulfilled her engagements as though nothing were happening. She went to Harrods to do her personal shopping, and altered nothing in her routine.

Then the King phoned her that he was going down to 'The Fort', which he thought wise, for all this trouble would soon pass. His mother may have made a last attempt to save things, but if she did she failed. She continued doing her job from Marlborough House. "Somebody must go on with the work," she told her ladies.

Life had treated Queen Mary badly. The death of the Duke of Clarence had been a horrifying experience, her marriage with King George difficult at times, for he could be very hard. Then came the loss of Prince John, whom she had adored. Now here was the worst blow of them all for, to her, David's conduct was a disgrace.

Her son told her again that he intended to marry Mrs Simpson the first moment that he could after the decree came through, and it was of little use for the Queen Mother once again to remind him, very gently, that the lady had been married twice already and had two husbands alive.

Whatever he felt about it, the Church of England does not approve of divorce, and to marry a third time in these circumstances was against that Church. But the fact that the King was the Head of that Church, and that the Church opposed him in this, appeared to make no difference. He had made up his mind to go through with it, to her grief, for she had never thought that he would. She curtseyed when he left her, never for a second did she forget that he was the King, but the whole affair seemed to be utterly hopeless. She appealed to him on behalf of Bertie, saying that she did not think that "Bertie could possibly do it, it asked too much of him". But he was adamant.

He said that he had only the one life to live and he had the right to live it in his own way, and marry the woman whom he loved. He would abdicate – the fateful word chilled her – and his brother would take over for him.

Mrs Simpson had already gone abroad.

She had been living with an aunt in London and the address had become known, with the result that she had experienced not only an unpleasant time, but a very alarming one when a mob stoned the house. She took off for Fort Belvedere, and then left England until things – as the King's friends hoped – settled themselves.

The King was afraid for her, and now it was all too plain to all the world that he was not going back on his word. He *would* abdicate and marry Wallis.

At Fort Belvedere in those crucial December days things moved fast and his mother knew that there was no going back.

At the signing of the Instrument of Abdication, the Duke of Kent – the brother closest to the King – broke down completely. He could not believe that his world had changed like this. It was, he said, one of the most ghastly moments in our history.

The night before he sailed away from his country for ever as King, the new Duke of Windsor told Ministers that he would broadcast to his country. They tried to deter him, but he was very obstinate, and said that he must and that he would. He would go 'on the air' from Windsor Castle.

He dined privately with the family. It could hardly have been

George V and Queen Mary in their Coronation robes, 1911

King Edward VIII, Queen Mary and other members of the Royal Family on the way to the Cenotaph for the Remembrance ceremony, November 1936

King Edward in South Wales, the month before his abdication, November 1936

a very happy dinner party whatever anyone said. His mother was there, quite tearless, and extremely brave, but she would suffer emotionally for this later. Then he went to broadcast from the castle.

It is one of the most famous speeches in the history of the land, and was beautifully delivered, with that sense of sadness which touched us all. He parted at midnight, springing into the waiting car, to leave for the Continent – as 'Mr James', a flashback to the last reigning Stuart. Under his arm he had tucked Mrs Simpson's little dog, which had been left behind to keep him company. He was driven to Portsmouth where HMS *Fury* was at his disposal. He was late, for there had been heavy fog on the road, and when he got there he tripped up the gangway, recognizing the captain standing there as a man (then cadet) whom he had known when they had been at Osborne together. They had not cared too much for one another then, and by the look on the captain's face he had not changed his mind about the former king.

He had gone, we believed, for ever.

That night the poor old Queen Mother wrote in her diary:

> The whole affair has lasted since November the sixteenth, and has been very painful, it is a terrific blow to all of us, particularly poor Bertie …

In this hour she must have suffered more than she had done in her whole life previously. The Princess Royal was in tears, for she could hardly believe it had happened. The King had conferred the Dukedom of Windsor on his brother but it was made clear that when he married Mrs Simpson would not assume the style of a 'royal highness', but simply a duchess.

The old Queen was wretched. Outwardly she took it calmly (very much Queen Mary) but she wept when alone. She was worried for the new King George VI's health. "But," she said, "he has a sweet wife, and that is the greatest help that a man can have."

In her diary she wrote, "We all feel very miserable."

But she went through all the engagements on her list, and lived her normal busy life. She wrote to David every week. Whatever he had done, she was still his mother, and would not go out of his life. They must have been difficult letters at first, but she steeled herself to write them.

The new monarch kept to the original date for the coronation, because a postponement would have affected too many people coming from abroad, and it was now that Queen Mary said that she wished to be present. This was a surprise! From apparently the time of the Plantagenets no Queen Mother had ever been present at the crowning of the new Sovereign, though why not she could not understand.

"I should *like* to be there," she said, "for, after all, he *is* my son."

Before the coronation Princess Mary slipped over to the Continent to visit her brother, who was very lonely, and possibly suffering badly as a result of the action he had taken. She was the first member of the Royal Family to propose a 'whip-round' for David.

This was the most difficult period of time for the new King, who was trying "to learn the job" as he put it. He also knew that his mother was not her old self. She had always been a very strong woman but the constitutional crisis had taken too much out of her.

"Life is hard to understand," she said, "and today it is not like it was when I was a girl."

This was too true. But she offered all her superb knowledge and help with the coming coronation, for she *was* the matriarch who knew.

Also she took her two little grand-daughters about London. "They must learn of our great city," she said. She adored the capital and knew it well, wanting Elizabeth and Margaret to remember what they saw and visiting with them places that she considered should be of importance to them. She never got tired; she was one of those women who could walk for miles, and usually did. She once said, "Going round hospitals taught me how to do it, and, believe me, *they* can be very tiring."

She took the children to Hampton Court Palace, the Tower of London, the Natural History Museum, the Victoria and Albert Museum, St Paul's Cathedral and Westminster Abbey. It gave her great joy.

She was so delighted that very slowly the country was recovering from the agony of the Abdication crisis, and she did hope that things were righting themselves.

The coronation had been arranged for 12th May 1937, but after a fairly good spring the weather failed, to the disappointment of all. It turned out to be cool and, at moments, wet. Nothing could have been more annoying for the huge crowd.

The Queen Mother, gloriously dressed, drove out of the palace gates, with a small princess on either side of her, both of them wearing diadems, to receive the most rousing welcome that she had ever had in all her life.

It was quite wonderful, she told others.

She looked magnificent and so erect, with that radiant smile of hers. Her reception from the understanding crowd must have cheered her immensely. In real life she was much better looking than her photographs made her, for in her portraits she usually looked stern, which she was not.

A private dinner had been held at the palace two days before the coronation, for the final discussion, and, as they talked, they heard the noise of the men hammering up the decorations into the night. I hope that the welcome which she got that day helped her. At the family dinner she had said, "Don't forget that we seldom get a fine day for a coronation, so don't be disappointed."

The Meteorological Office had forecast damp weather, which was putting it mildly, for the rain came on quite heavily!

The ceremony was, as ever, magnificent, and was broadcast. Perhaps one of the most marvellous high spots was when the new Queen Consort curtseyed to the new King. Her train was carried by six daughters of peers and, approaching the throne, they all dropped together into the most magnificent combined curtsey, which was quite remarkable!

Driving along with her grandmother, little Princess Margaret had great trouble with her coronet which kept slipping. She wanted to look from side to side, and the coronet could not take it. I think the great joy of the coronation, indicating that despite the Abdication the throne was as stable as ever, helped the Queen Mother a little. It was like old times. And waving to the crowds and trying to keep Princess Margaret's coronet on her head kept her busy. She felt that her world was recovering its spirits. But her chief worry was her eldest son.

Mrs Simpson was living in France, under her first married name of Warfield, and apparently the Duke of Windsor was very anxious to get a Church of England clergyman to officiate. This was not too easy, for the Church of England was not so pleased with him, as he found. He wrote to some parsons, who declined, but in the end he found a clergyman who volunteered, and his offer was eagerly accepted. The clergyman accordingly set sail for France and duly married the Duke to his Duchess at the Château de Candé on 3rd June three weeks after the coronation.

I am sure that his mother must have been hurt by the newspapers for the whole affair had upset her far more than she ever admitted. It had hurt her dreadfully, for to her the Abdication had been unspeakable. Nevertheless one was a mother, and she telegraphed her congratulations to David.

But she did recognize the fact that her second son would be a far more reliable sovereign, and England would benefit enormously by the change, if only his health would stand up to it, and this both she and Mrs Bill doubted.

Mrs Bill told me that she thought it would kill him for he was very loyal and would overwork rather than neglect his duties.

"But he isn't strong enough for the life of a King," said Mrs Bill, "and I *do* know that."

The Queen Mother was enchanted over the ultimate success of the lessons taken by Bertie to prevent stammering. Thanks to the ministrations of an Australian, Lionel Logue, he spoke much better and had stopped being nervous about it. The joy and strain of the coronation was over and done with, and the season was ending when the first warning of trouble from Germany came to us.

There was a dictator there called Adolf Hitler, a strange man whom some said was mad, but he had done a tremendous lot for his country which had lost the war. The Italian Mussolini had been the first of the big dictators, but people said that Adolf Hitler was running him close. He had got Germany into a stage of recovery from the humiliation of defeat. The Germans had been through a stark time and had longed for a leader, and then, quite suddenly, this man had appeared. Now we became aware that there could be danger here, for Germany had secretly re-armed.

Queen Mary disliked the very word 'dictator', of course, and when Britain awakened to the fact that danger could be unpleasantly close to us, we all hoped that the reports from Germany were wildly exaggerated. They were not.

"It never does to believe gossip," the Queen Mother said. "Most of it is exaggerated" – which was true, but I think that she must have been very anxious over the changes in Europe.

Civil war had come to Spain, and that had lasted for nearly three years. King Alfonso and Queen Ena were dethroned, and escaped, but they must have had a most difficult escape. The restlessness in Europe (and it seemed to be almost everywhere) had blinded us to the fact that Germany was arming to an alarming extent.

Of course, the Foreign Office knew all about Adolf Hitler. Mussolini had also been a menace, but the man in the street did not give the strident Italian a second thought. Germany had at one time been brought to its knees, and now it had somehow come out of that agony and seemed to be quite strong. It worried the Queen Mother. She felt that one could not trust the Nazis.

Again, she had not been at all well. She could not put the abdication completely behind her. She went down to Sandringham again to visit the people whom she loved down there, and the old faithful servants – "doing the rounds" was what she called it.

The air always helped her; she vowed that there was nothing in the world like Norfolk air, and she visited Mrs Bill several times. They were devoted to each other, and possibly Mrs Bill knew more about the Queen Mother than anybody else in the world.

She went shopping, too, around the antique shops in King's Lynn, displaying the knowledge of an expert; nobody could sell her a 'fake'. "Well, that is something that I *do* know," she would say with that gay little laugh, for she could still laugh like a young girl. But she was ageing and it irritated her; she complained that it was so sickening, having always done everything, and now finding that she could not cope. "I forget the very things that I know quite well," she said, "and it is so maddening."

One might have thought that the fact that her husband had died at Sandringham House, his elder brother before him, would have deterred her, but she never lost her deep affection for the place. The children had been young there, and she had come to York Cottage as a bride. To her it was still home.

This trouble with Germany – she felt we could never have another war, for in the last one the flower of England had died. There could never be any more fighting with them, surely?

Unhappily, none could reassure her. In 1937 it had become plain that Hitler had war mania and would do anything for power. He was another Bonaparte. The future looked black.

Naturally the downtrodden Germans had the greatest faith in their new leader, if only because he was a leader, and they would do anything to better their future. It was then that England woke up to the fact that something was very wrong. Perhaps because we had defeated the Kaiser we had felt sure that there could never be another war, for had not 1914-18 been the war to end all wars?

Now we realized danger threatened us.

The Queen Mother said, rather sadly, that she thought there would always be wars. We had overlooked the fact that there are men like Napoleon, men of the people, who rise suddenly, lead for a time and bring terrible suffering with them.

Queen Mary felt that Europe had changed so much since she was a girl that perhaps she was rather old-fashioned.

"I'm getting old," she thought, "and the whole world has changed so much that it is difficult to keep pace with it."

Too many crowns had already fallen. Europe was not what it was.

She had never been very sure of Germany and she said so. She did not feel that they were a trustworthy nation; she felt that the Kaiser deserved everything that he got, and now it seemed that Germany was reverting to type.

The awful thought of another war in Europe with Britain involved rumbled for a time, then suddenly it blazed into action with startling suddenness. Hitler was not the nice, fond-of-little children man he had posed as being. He was even stronger than the swaggering Mussolini had been. By 1938 we knew this, knew to our cost that this man Hitler enjoyed quite immense power. In 1938 a crisis flared up, and suddenly it seemed almost as if we had blinded ourselves to the truth for undoubtedly Germany was almost ready for war.

When we went into the matter it appeared that he had an enormous army, and we had *not*. The crisis over Czechoslovakia is not one which anybody who lived through it is likely to forget. Although for the moment we got through it (and that was a miracle) perhaps it would have been better for all concerned if we had gone to war then and there and had taken him by surprise. Germany was not at that time absolutely ready for battle.

The Queen Mother, used to England's greatness and power, was absolutely wretched about it. The trouble was, were we strong enough to fight? She remembered last time when we had been really strong and felt so sure that we were certain of winning, even then it had been a dreadful war. Now, with this new man in command, we were facing a far stronger enemy, and if there *was* a war we *could* lose it. Could England's greatness disappear?

"That is impossible," she said with superb calm, but she must have known that need not be true.

Those in power argued that they had been so sure of peace that they could afford to let some things go a little. The King was resolute that there must not be a war, but how to stop it was quite another story.

Princess Mary was now spending much time with her mother at Marlborough House. The years had seemed to increase the age gap between her and her husband. The time had come when she realized that Queen Mary needed her, for she was ill, though the public did not know this. The Princess had gone to nurse her. The Queen was a good, obedient patient, accepting orders implicitly, but the trouble over Edward VIII and the anxiety (now showing itself) about the rule of Adolf Hitler in Germany had not helped her.

She missed the Derby – a race which she loved; she was always given a most tremendous reception at Epsom. She turned up at Ascot, but she admitted that she tired far too easily, something that was new to her for she had been practically tireless before this. The doctors wanted her to go out and about. She was a woman who loved people, and the more that she saw of them the better it was for her.

At the end of the season she returned to Sandringham and only now did she realize what a tremendous lot it had always meant to her. Her first home had been here. It looked rather small these days, she told herself, she wondered how she had managed in it.

"I'm getting older," she told the old servants whom she visited. "It comes on you so quietly that you don't notice it at first, do you? I'm not so good on my feet."

She had been through utter misery as Mrs Bill said, for she told me: "I don't think that she ever recovered from the abdication and the horror that it was to her. That was dreadful!"

She also found dictatorship difficult to understand as did most crowned heads of course. The Hitler crisis came with appalling suddenness.

All at once it seemed that the fate of Europe was again hanging in the balance. The Queen Mother went in person to the House of Commons to hear Mr Chamberlain make his statement there. She was desperately anxious about it all, for she felt that this was the worst crisis we had ever had to face. Whilst Mr Chamberlain was actually making his speech, he was interrupted to be handed a message that had come from Germany.

This was the Führer's reply to his inquiry earlier in the day, and the message was that Adolf Hitler would see him again tomorrow afternoon. In a way the Prime Minister must have been delighted with this ray of hope, but horrified at the thought of meeting Adolf Hitler yet again, for the first interview in Munich had been terrible.

When the pair of them had met for the first time Hitler had shrieked and raged like a madman. Mr Chamberlain had indeed thought that he was mad, but it seemed here was a breathing space, and he was completely surprised by it. Queen Mary wrote in her diary:

> I was myself so much moved, that I could not speak to any of the ladies in the gallery. Several of them, then though unknown to me, seized my hand. It was very touching. Let us now pray that a lasting peace may follow.

She was not an emotional woman; she never gave the impression of caring deeply for others, of her gaiety of spirit and of her understanding. But I think she *did* appreciate that Mr Chamberlain had had a ghastly time with the Führer. And back he came with, so we believed, peace in his pocket!

I shall never forget the enormous crowd outside Buckingham Palace that night, and the thrill when Mr Chamberlain's car came through and we thought he had peace in the bag. It was the famous Munich Agreement, not worth the paper on which it was written, of course, but England was rapturous! What cheering when the Queen Mother and the King and Queen and Mr Chamberlain came on to the palace balcony. It was the loudest I have ever heard.

We are saved, was what it sounded like.

Like us, I feel that she believed this was peace. At that time none of us realized that we were dealing with a megalomaniac. An eccentric we thought, but not a real madman. I do not believe that the man was ever sane.

On the top of this the Queen Mother got a nasty attack of laryngitis and had to retire to bed. She hated time catching up with her, and said so. She had never been ill, or ailing, and possibly did not realize that she had suffered far too great a strain, for which she was now paying.

All her troubles came together.

Her sister-in-law, Queen Maud of Norway, of whom Queen Mary was very fond, had to have an operation and came to London for it. Queen Mary went to visit her at a famous nursing home the day before, and they had a long talk with lots of memories to recall, and they could discuss matters heart-to-heart. The Queen of Norway had her operation next day; the report was that everything was satisfactory, but she died three days later. This distressed Queen Mary very much indeed.

"We played together as children," she wrote in a letter to a friend, and of course this is a tie throughout one's life. "We knew one another so well."

It hurt her that she had come to the time of life when too many friends fade away and, as she once said to her husband, "There is never anyone who quite takes their places, and today it is such a different and difficult world."

The old year died and snow came almost at Christmas; although most people thought that Mr Chamberlain had made a lasting peace in 1938, Queen Mary distrusted Hitler, and had done from the first. His was a dangerous fanaticism and, of course, she possibly knew of many of the disturbing things that were happening in Europe.

We had not gone far into the spring of 1939 before bad news came. Hitler's army was on the move, with the intention of overrunning Europe in the long run. He was copying Napoleon and there seemed to be no limits to his aggression. His power increased as he progressed, and now all England was getting very worked up.

The January of that year was the last calm month we were to have for years. We had flattered ourselves that it would be peace, and now Hitler's army had taken the whole of Czechoslovakia, and was rampaging on for more.

Queen Mary was horrified. A hopeless sense of frustration seized the country, and although we had all said that another war was unthinkable, what choice had we?

The King and Queen went that summer to the United States on a state visit. This was in the May, and they started in the most glorious weather. The Queen Mother was left in charge of the two little princesses, and she sympathized with her son and also with her daughter-in-law going away, for she knew the tremendous fatigue imposed by these visits, of which one of the worst aspects was that never for a single second must one show how tiring it all is. She saw them off, the little princesses with her, and until they had departed she concealed her fears for the future fate of Europe. Queen Mary herself was a clever politician; she knew more about the situation than most women, and also knew more of the dangers. Sooner or later she felt that war *must* come, and then what?

The North American visit went far better than anyone had anticipated. When she left England one might have thought that the little Queen Elizabeth was putting on weight; certainly it seemed like it. But after an arduous if triumphal tour from coast to coast across Canada she was much slimmer when the royal party crossed the border at Niagara into the United States of America (to the wildest cheering anyone had ever heard). With her loss of weight she looked almost as she had done as a girl.

America, like Canada, fell for her in a very big way.

At home the Queen Mother was enchanted. "I *knew* they'd

love her," was what she said. And she was happy for Bertie – the first British reigning monarch ever to visit the United States.

While the King and Queen were away, however, she became the reluctant cause of family anxiety. She was fulfilling many public engagements during the Sovereign's absence and one day as usual she set off in the official car, a stately limousine, with two companions in attendance. Returning from Wimbledon, the car was struck by a heavy lorry and overturned.

Lord Claud Hamilton, her Comptroller, and Lady Constance Milnes Gaskell, her Woman of the Bedchamber, were flung on the floor in a heap, together with their royal mistress. Broken glass from the windows poured in on them, like rain. It must have been a ghastly shock! It must also have been a surprise for a local doctor, when he found who his patient was and, although she remained completely calm, for she never lost her head, she was terribly shaken. She was rescued from the car on a ladder which – according to an eye-witness – she negotiated without a tremor, not a hair out of place.

But she was dreadfully bruised, and getting her out of the wrecked limousine was an ordeal for the rescuers, especially when they recognized her, still sedate and outwardly unmoved in one of her famous toques.

All her engagements had to be cancelled immediately, much to her annoyance, for she insisted that a couple of days in bed would put her right. She had always been an optimist! This time it meant more than a couple of days. She took longer than she thought to recover properly. Used to superb good health, she did not understand being ill, and had never had an accident in her whole life before this. When it came she started to wonder.

"I'm getting too old," she said to the doctors, "and, as you grow older, life becomes more difficult. Things go wrong."

But she rejoiced in the magnificent tour that the King and Queen were making in the United States. They proved to be wildly popular. The King was now far more sure of his speech, hardly stammering at all, which was a help. The Queen Mother rejoiced in their success, and in their accounts of their visits with the presidential Roosevelts, but she was troubled about the rumours of war with Germany.

She prayed that something would stop it, but Hitler seemed bent on taking countries across Europe and, in the end, our turn would surely come unless he was stopped. She wished we were back in the old times of her youth when we had so much.

Everything has changed out of all knowledge, she told herself, and I cannot *bear* to think of yet another war. We would lose too much.

10

War and the Move to Badminton

Possibly this period of waiting for a war which we all felt must come imposed the heaviest burden of all. During the suspense of the Munich crisis, Queen Mary's presentiment persisted. Mr Chamberlain had come home with nothing more than a piece of waste paper in his hand (not what we had felt when it happened – the end of a bitter crisis, and no war ever again). Now it was clear to the Queen Mother that war was only a matter of time.

The old Queen said she had recovered from the very nasty car accident far better than she had thought possible, and she felt that she might yet emulate her grandmother who had lived to be ninety-three years old.

About this time she was giving sittings for an effigy of herself which was destined ultimately to go with the late King's monument. This, one would have thought, was a most gruesome experience for her, but she took it quite casually. She never lost her tremendous self-control. It was she who had asked the sculptor to do it whilst she was still there to sit for it and, when he demurred, she urged him on.

"Nothing hurries death" was what she said, and she accepted the sittings quite calmly as part of the day's work. She said to him, "None of this can make me die a single day sooner – or later if it comes to that!"

Dying never worried her. She was a very religious woman who adhered to her faith, and this was comforting, of course. But she hated the thought of another war coming, even though she had often said when the first war ended that it was not the last one.

Now Hitler was literally invading the whole of Europe. Mussolini attacked Albania. He had been threatening it for some time, but had held back, and now, seeing how his friend and ally Hitler was progressing, he seized the chance.

Queen Mary had very much liked King Zog and Queen Geraldine of Albania when they met, and was horrified to hear they had been forced to flee their country, and with a son and heir only two days old.

As the inevitable hour approached, the King had to plan for his mother's safety. She certainly could not remain at Marlborough House, and most certainly she could not stay at Sandringham, as it was far too near the east coast, and there would be air attacks. It was hard to find a suitable place for her.

Adolf Hitler – "that hateful fiend" she called him – had the power to bomb London if he wished (and he *would* wish), and if she stayed at Marlborough House she would be a sitting target, of course. Her family thought the West Country might be the safest place for her. She herself was not concerned for her safety, and did not want any preferential treatment. She wished to stay in her own country, of course, and with the people she had reigned over. Courage was always her strong point, for she was particularly brave. The King talked with her, pointing out gently that those who were protecting her would need a safer place than Sandringham.

Balmoral was one place they had thought of, but the Queen Mother had not the same devotion to Scotland as Queen Victoria had had.

Various suggestions were made, but in the end they decided on the Duke of Beaufort's seat at Badminton in Gloucestershire. Queen Mary made no demur. The Duchess was her niece, the daughter of her eldest brother Adolphus (Dolly).

Meanwhile in London she was fitted with a gas mask, as

Queen Mary with the Princesses Elizabeth and Margaret in 1939

Mrs Bill, nanny to Queen Mary's children

Four generations of the Royal Family: Queen Mary, King George VI, Princess Elizabeth holding Princess Anne (whose christening photograph this is), the Duke of Edinburgh and Queen Elizabeth the Queen Mother holding Prince Charles everyone had been when we stood on the brink of hostilities, and every one of us hoping that, at the last moment, something would happen to stop the war.

Towards the end of August she went to the House of Commons to hear Mr Chamberlain's speech.

"This is the most dreadful thing that has ever happened," she said when war was declared on 3rd September, and very soon after there was an air raid warning, which alarmed everyone, though no shot was fired, no bomb dropped, and nothing happened.

"War is always dreadful," she said, and was glad that the little princesses were at Balmoral with Crawfie, their governess, and only prayed that, somehow or other, we should get out of this ghastly war.

She finally left London for Badminton House, in that strange interlude which her contemporaries called 'the phoney war'. Was Hitler already going back on it, they asked, and trying to get out of it?

Those in power knew a very different story.

The Queen Mother took the decision to leave London with her usual philosophical composure. She felt she should stay in London, even as an example to others, but she *did* realize that, if there was heavy bombing, she would be a great liability, and as an example to other older people she ought to go. This was the war that we had to win or perish, and she knew it. How she hated leaving the capital which had been the centre of her public activities for years! But her safety and the peace of mind of her advisers were involved.

The effort of packing her things was prodigious. It was going to be a long war (she knew it herself), and possibly she would be away for years.

The Duke of Beaufort had already joined up, so it was the Duchess who received her aunt on her arrival.

I am sure that the Queen Mother was wretched, for she called her evacuation "fleeing before the enemy".

I always feel that she must have been a difficult guest, for with her she brought sixty servants, which was no small order. She had, of course, always liked country life, but, as she said, she had never before "been banished".

That first winter was a long and dreary period, aggravated by the fact that nothing seemed to be happening in the war. There were none of the predicted vicious air attacks; and where at the beginning everybody had been asking, "How long do you think the war will last?" now the one question was, "When do you think the war is going to start?"

It would have been something of a joke, save that under the feeling of make-believe lurked the fear that something nasty lay ahead.

The Queen Mother found Badminton rather dull after "dear old Sandringham". She knitted vigorously, and made friends with the villagers who at first had been wary of her but soon came to appreciate her homely virtues.

"I feel that I am doing nothing," she said to those who visited her, "and I ought to be doing so much."

I saw her when staying at Bath in the spring of 1940, before the war had really started. The royal car drew up outside Forte's, where they sell the famous Bath buns, and a gentleman-in-waiting went inside, coming out again with a small paper bag of buns. The Queen Mother looked well, I thought. She was enormously interested in the antique shops in Bath, and her deep knowledge impressed the dealers. A man who kept one of them laughed as he said: "She is not a lady you can deceive. She knows what is what when she sees it."

But her first duty, she felt, was to break the silence with the villagers and the tenants on the great Badminton estate. She would ask them how many children they had, and told them, "I had six and I would have loved to have had another daughter."

She had a bedroom on the first floor at Badminton, with a sitting-room which had the most glorious view of the park stretching into the distance. She used the Oak Room as a drawing-room, and entertained people there when they came to pay their respects.

"It is quiet but very lovely here," she said, but she *was* homesick for her family and for London. The King sent her confidential documents to keep her abreast of affairs, but it was not the same as being at the heart of things, and she realized wistfully that her entire world had completely altered.

"But, then, so has everybody else's world," she said. "I am not the only person who has had to leave home; men are joining up everywhere and wives and children are left to do as best they can. Everybody is suffering in some way or another. Let's hope it is not for long."

When she did meet her son the King, she felt a mother's concern because she thought that he looked quite ill. Nobody realized how much he had to do. She told him she was lonely, which she was, and she hated not being 'in the news'. It was this 'confession' which enabled the King to change things for her – and instantly. On his instructions the Foreign Office arranged for the latest inside intelligence to be sent down to his mother, in a red dispatch box. This kind thought helped her enormously. She felt somehow that she was doing something; it was almost like old times! She had told her son that she was entirely out of touch or so she felt, and it was a strange experience after years of being *in* touch with the whole world. But having a dispatch box daily changed her attitude, and, as she was able to interpret affairs intelligently, her interest in the outside world revived and she was often able to offer useful advice.

She also took great interest in the beautiful gardens at Badminton and asked if she could occasionally 'give a hand'. A number of the Beaufort gardeners had been called up, and, after all, Queen Mary *had* gardened at home.

"It will never do to let that ivy become master of the situation," she told her hostess, "and I would love to have a go at it."

Ivy had attacked the brickwork of the Palladian mansion.

With the Queen Mother's help it was rendered harmless.

Evacuation of the countryside also had compensations. The young Duke of Kent was able to visit her fairly frequently; he held the rank of Air Commodore. One of his duties was to inspect RAF stations, so he flew to the West Country from time to time and always called on his mother when he was there. They were a most devoted pair, and always had been, from the time when they had danced Highland reels together most vigorously.

Some said that he was her favourite son, though she was a lady who did not encourage favourites, but she found the Prince an enjoyable companion on these occasions, as he broke the monotony of life away from the world, and brought her bits of news. He had always had a most sparkling gift of chatter, which helped her enormously, and he was amusingly gay.

In 1940 everyone thought the war would either fizzle out (Hitler having found that he had bitten off more than he could chew) or that, quite suddenly, it would blow up – and it did the latter.

"It will end with one violent battle," some forecast. There they were entirely wrong. Possibly this long, dreary time when nothing happened at all was the worst, for nobody could think what Adolf Hitler was doing.

He gave the impression of regretting that he had ever come into the war, for not a single shot was fired west of the Rhine.

It was with the new spring, and the lengthening days that it all began. The air raid warning wailed, and after that it stopped for only brief intervals. In Europe the Nazis overran countries with unprecedented speed.

It horrified the old Queen when she saw a picture of Queen Juliana and Prince Bernhard of the Netherlands at Liverpool Street station, having come here for help, and realized that yet another crown had toppled (if only temporarily). She was not so much concerned for herself ("I am old and no longer of any real use to the country" was the way that she put it), but she was horrified to read of the beautiful buildings which were being simply mown down and of the precious possessions lost.

"People change," she said, "they die, and leave you, but beautiful belongings are always beautiful and these can never be replaced."

That first spring of the war when suddenly the naked truth of Germany's might burst upon us was perhaps the worst time that we had to endure, because it was such a surprise. It had been a completely silent winter, which had given us much encouragement, and now, in a single day, we suddenly learnt that maybe we had not understood this man Hitler at all, and there was going to be a real war.

Far from Adolf Hitler's having bitten off more than he could chew (which was what we had thought), it was he who had waited for the good weather to start and, when it began, he opened up with a vengeance.

This was the springtime of unfortunate reality. Queen Mary thought that Hitler had behaved like the old Napoleon, only he seemed cleverer. She maintained that the only thing to do was to remain staunch and have confidence in our leaders. Also to remember that this country has the amazing advantage of being an island. It would be difficult to invade. She showed no apprehension or dismay during the war, but only the eager desire to help.

She had settled down in Badminton. The King wondered whether she would not have been safer at Windsor Castle with the princesses, but that would have increased the security problem, bombproof though the castle might be.

The Queen Mother told him that "it happened to be just a matter of luck", and added that nobody could run away from death, for in the end it always caught up with you. He was not quite convinced.

She was not nervous, or anxious and, besides, ever since she had been a girl she had loved pottering about gardens, pulling up a dandelion here or groundsel there. Naturally her host was not too pleased to see the Queen Mother doing what she called "a good spot of weeding".

Then the unexpected happened. An unexploded bomb fell on somebody's potato patch, behind the village post office. Instantly everyone was at action stations. The bomb disposal unit came out from Bristol at speed, and the unwelcome visitor was rendered harmless.

"It is all right," Queen Mary telephoned her son. "I rang up because I thought you might be a bit worried."

He was not at all sure that she *was* all right, and he sent a military guard down to Badminton for his mother. More than a hundred men of the Gloucestershire Regiment were placed on this special duty. The authorities felt that in the event of an enemy invasion she would need protection.

However, Queen Mary still maintained: "They will never invade England. You'll see that I was right about this." She had flashes of intuition, and often made predictions which time proved to be absolutely true. She had forecast accurately what would happen if her eldest son decided to marry.

As she aged she had more and more of what she called "peeps into the future". They never worried her; in fact, she said that they helped her. Perhaps she thought that the great griefs of her life had passed her by, and she was accordingly a little more content.

But she felt there were other troubles awaiting her and, sadly, she was right. On rare occasions she went to London, and had lunch at Buckingham Palace, which made her feel that she was home again. It was there that she found a little red flower was actually sprouting and blossoming in Bond Street wreckage; she could scarcely believe the evidence of her eyes.

(Ancestors of this attractive little plant were first noted growing among the ruins after the Great Fire of London in 1666.)

She hated the gaps where houses had gone, and shuddered that the house the Yorks had loved so much in Piccadilly had been damaged.

"It is all quite horrible," she said. "I cannot bear to think that this is happening to our dear, dear country."

She returned sadly to Badminton, reflecting that the capital city was no place for her. But it worried her that the family were still there, for she feared anything could happen, not excluding the fact that the King and other members of the Royal Family ran a real risk of being kidnapped by enemy paratroops.

Back at Badminton she resumed her own special "war of the ivy". She loved having a worthwhile job to do.

In August 1942 the Queen Mother visited Windsor (she told a friend that none would ever know how much she had missed it) for the baptism of her latest Kent grandson for whom she had knitted hard. On the 4th he was christened Michael George Charles Franklin (the last after his godfather, President Roosevelt). She also went to Coppins, which had been left to them by the late Princess Victoria, her husband's sister. The Queen Mother had been enchanted by this legacy. The lovely old mansion at Iver, near Windsor, was just what they wanted most.

"Coppins is a charming house, and it has a glorious garden for the children," she said.

The raids had eased off at this time; she was not disturbed whilst there, and in her diary she wrote:

> Georgie is so happy with his lovely wife and the dear baby.

The bombing of London, as she was able to confirm from later visits, had been far worse than she had guessed, and she could not think how it would ever recover. After seeing some of the damage she could not imagine how people had lived through it. But, as she said, Britons never lacked when it came to courage. They were brave as lions always when it came to war.

But it saddened her to see beautiful houses in ruins, and streets she had known completely changed by the debris and the general wreckage lying there. We shall pull through, she said, but all this *will* take time.

On these visits the King would not let her stay very long. To one of her ladies she said, with a laugh, "I am being treated like a parcel. An air raid is no worse for me than it is for anybody else, and I'd like to stay longer."

But the King would not have this. The capital was no place for the very young, or the very old, and realizing how he felt about it, she did not press her request. Perhaps she was ageing a little. She tired more easily. Who wouldn't, with a war on?

"One never realizes how old one is," she told one of her ladies a trifle sorrowfully. "Age creeps up behind you and suddenly you find that you can't do what you did before. It is something of a shock. It all came so easily once."

She wept for London; could it ever be quite the same again? she asked herself. At heart she was entirely a Londoner, but she did appreciate that her son had been quite right when he had insisted that she went away. London was no place for her now. She could at best be only a visitor.

"I wish this had not come with my old age," she said. "I could have done so much more to help at one time, and now, I ... well, I can't."

It was a dreadful admission but she had to make it.

She was comparatively safe and on the whole happy at Badminton which reminded her of her early days at White Lodge. She could not stay sitting about with her knitting for ever, and she said so. She had to have some work to do, proper work, she told them.

11

Another Bereavement

But it was too long a war.

She said nothing, nobody ever heard her complain, but she ached to be back in London, at the heart of things, and what she called "doing something for the country, not just fiddling about like this". She had retained her dominant personality throughout all her troubles.

Meanwhile she had made many friends among the cottagers and tenants; she was interested in the way they made the wartime food rations go round, their gardens and their children. She was a woman of wide outside interests, never an introvert.

Constantly she heard the sirens going, but, as she said to her ladies, "I suppose one gets used to them."

She realized that of course the Germans knew her location exactly, but apparently they were ignoring her, and she felt she ought to be thankful for that.

Her host and hostess were worried that she would tire herself out attacking the ivy as she did; she really made the most splendid job of it, and enjoyed getting on with it. She was a very practical personality who had been brought up to work, and she adored "doing something for others".

There were air raids all around her, but she never showed any fear of them, only anxiety for the people who might lose everything through them. She had an implicit belief in God.

She went to local concerts, bazaars and meetings, and enjoyed them. She very much wanted to help. All her life she had been one of the busiest servants of the State, poor lady, and now she missed having a real job to do. Like many other women in the land she found the long evenings of winter trying, and hated the wailing note of the siren, telling her that the enemy was here again.

"I shall never get used to that siren," she said, "but perhaps that is happening to everybody." In the summer Badminton was lovely, but the winter was not the same story, and as she said once to a friend: "The winter seems to last such a very long time, doesn't it?"

She knew from her dispatch box which arrived daily that the war was not going well. She took all the newspapers that she could get and supplemented their censored information with the facts in her box. She was trusted, the woman who had never betrayed a secret in her life and never would.

"It really is a ghastly war," she said. She had not cared for the Kaiser when he had visited them for the unveiling of the Victoria Memorial, but she thought that Hitler was worse! Once, stirred by news of some atrocious violence of his, she said: "I shall never understand why that man was allowed to be born!"

From her private papers she could not see the end of the war for a long time, or the prospect of anyone's winning or losing it.

"It'll go on for ever," she said, then laughed: "But in the end it will come out all right. One has to trust the leaders. Churchill is wonderful; he'll get a victory one day."

She wrote regularly to her eldest son, now Governor of the Bahamas; they had corresponded from the week when he had left the country for exile. "I am his mother," was what she said, and she added: "Even if the whole world deserts him, that is something that I shall never do. A man needs his mother, whatever his age is. I am sure of that."

She felt sure that he needed her more now than he had ever done before, and, whatever happened, nothing changed the fact that he *was* her son. She was his mother to the end. "I love all my children," she said. That was the sort of loyalty that she had always practised, for it was ingrained.

But the crown should have come first. She would never

understand how he had come to renounce it. She herself could never have done it, but she tried to forget that. So she wrote him regularly, and he always replied to her letters. *He was still her son.*

The sadness that had always haunted her had not ended yet. She had said once or twice, "Something more will happen, I feel it within me." Although her ladies tried to get her away from this premonition, it lingered on.

One evening after dinner, when she had returned to her sitting-room, she ran out of knitting wool, and her lady-in-waiting went to fetch more.

The telephone rang, and she herself answered it. Perhaps that was one of the most terrible moments of her whole life, for she was immediately put through to the King himself, who told her what had happened.

That evening – only three weeks after Prince Michael's christening – the Duke of Kent had been flying to Iceland, as she knew. He had told her only the other day, when he had been here to lunch with her, and afterwards they had gone out to look at the Badminton ivy together.

There had been an accident. "He isn't hurt?" she gasped.

The awful truth was that his warplane had crashed into the Scottish hills not far from Balmoral, killing all but one survivor.

She listened in that dreadful silence which comes when one is most terribly affected by ill news. Already she had endured far too much, for she had always been the victim of the most cruel circumstances – her fiancé within six weeks of their coming marriage; her youngest son; her husband; and then the agony of the abdication. Could any woman have taken more? At this very moment, also, she was worried about the King himself, for Bertie was losing weight rather badly, and suffered from an ominous little cough that she did not like at all.

Queen Mary sat there in the lofty sitting-room as one turned to stone in a torment of suspense. To herself she kept saying: "It can't be true. It can't be true." The lady-in-waiting, returning with the wool, saw her at the telephone and dutifully withdrew again.

The Duke of Kent was the Queen Mother's youngest surviving son, a happy extrovert, quite the most attractive member of the Royal Family, and in an instant she remembered how his story-book romance with Princess Marina had warmed the heart of the nation. They were a most popular couple.

"It can't be true," the poor old Queen said over and over again.

George would not have suffered, thank God, which was comforting, for it was all over before he could have known anything about it. The one survivor who had stumbled about in the heather dazed and lost for hours before he was rescued, confirmed that the aircraft was off course. It was an extremely dark night. There was fog about. Death would have come in a split second. No time to think.

The Queen Mother, pale and shocked, could not believe that the handsome young Prince who had been joking around in the ivy with her only a few days back in the park was now no more.

"We laughed a lot," she remembered; and now the memory had the power to wound her. Then her thoughts flew to his wife.

"I hope somebody has gone to Marina at once," she said.

The King had thought of this already and even as Queen Mary was recalling her last meeting with George, someone was on the way to Coppins. This was a dreadful shock for everybody, and quite unexpected, coming as it did out of the blue. Queen Mary thought of the new baby – born on America's Independence Day, which was why President Roosevelt was invited to be his godfather – and told herself: "He'll never remember his father, which is quite dreadful." Prince George had been the merriest of them all, the boy who had never tired of dancing reels, and could run anybody out at cricket. Now he was dead, the beautiful Princess Marina a widow and her three children fatherless.

"I'm getting older," she thought, "for this has cut deeper than anything has gone before, even when David left us," and she tried desperately to pull herself together.

She needed all her courage, for this loss had affected her very badly, and she aged considerably in a matter of days. Now, when she spoke, her voice had the first frailty of old age in it, a quavering note which had not been there before. She tried to conceal her weakness, and her ladies understood her and did everything they could for her. They wanted to help, but it is hard to console when death is so terribly final.

"As though we had not had sufficient without this as well," she said.

On the night of the fatality she refused to go to bed until she had written a note to Princess Marina, for she had never shirked an unpleasant duty in her life, and she was not starting now.

I personally think that she never recovered from the shock of the Duke of Kent's death. She made prodigious efforts to preserve her immaculate self-control, but her calm for once deserted her as she burst out "*How* could they run into a mountain?" The country were waiting to know the answer to this question.

The Royal Family were utterly shocked and some people said that Queen Mary was never quite the same again, but with a stoicism that astonished the Court she announced firmly that, whatever was said to the contrary, she intended to attend the funeral at Windsor.

It was her greatest sorrow (she admitted it), for the two of them had often laughed together (and he, like his mother, had the most infectious laugh); and now he had gone for ever. She had lost his brightness, the quality in him that she had always loved.

Her children did not want her to attend the funeral. They feared, firstly, that already she had suffered too much and, secondly, that it would be too moving for her.

Then there was the fear that undoubtedly the Germans would somehow find out when and where it was taking place, and it would be a grand opportunity for them to plan a giant air raid, and bomb the castle whilst they were in St George's Chapel.

But Queen Mary was adamant.

"I shall attend the funeral," she said, and they had to accept this, a royal command backed with all the force of her considerable personality.

On 29th August the whole Royal Family assembled for the obsequies: all through the previous night the body of the Duke of Kent had rested in the memorial chapel, where, years back, the Queen Mother's fiancé, the Duke of Clarence, had lain awaiting burial.

The misery of that memory must have caused the ageing Queen Mother deep anguish, but she never shed a single tear.

In the end the young Duke's body did not remain in the crypt of St George's Chapel alongside so many of our kings and queens. His widow knew that he had always hated the idea of this; the whole of the Royal Family disliked that crypt. It was a gruesome place, and over-crowded, too. A new ground for burial had been prepared at Frogmore, near the royal mausoleum where Queen Victoria and her beloved Albert lay. Here was a lovely garden with green grass and a charming little stream running through it, with flowers everywhere.

So, a little later on, the body of the Prince was removed from the crypt early one spring morning, and taken to Frogmore before the rest of the country was awake. (Some years later the body of his favourite brother, the Duke of Windsor, was brought from France to lie near him at Frogmore, for he had hated the original crypt as well.)

It was quite a time before the bereaved Queen Mother returned to tearing down the ivy at Badminton. She had difficulty in recovering from this shock, and for a while seemed to lose her interest in life.

Now the Princess Royal came to live permanently with her. The marriage with the big age difference had not become any the happier, for Harewood was very aloof in his ways and people said he had always been difficult. Perhaps if the Princess had had a daughter the bond would have been stronger, but she had borne two sons, and they, in turn, never produced a grand-daughter for her.

Queen Mary remained at Badminton until the last shot was fired. Britain had come through quite the most difficult war in her history. It had been brought about by a madman. In the end nobody questioned that madness, for it was there for all the world to see.

12

A Marriage and a Great-grandson

She was tremendously proud of her son the King and all that he had done. We had come through the most difficult war, we hoped the last one in our history – if one can ever do without wars, and the ageing Queen Mary did not believe this possible. A maniac had started this one, and there would always be 'fiends' of that kind. She listened to her son's victory broadcast, surprised and delighted at his relaxed manner, for his speech had improved enormously.

She felt that he had had an exhausting time. He had been made to receive the crown which his elder brother had literally thrown away, then faced one of the most cruel wars in our history, if not the cruellest.

She stayed on in the country for a little while to attend the village peace celebrations at the Portcullis Club, which was part of the local inn, and always catered for affairs of this kind. She sat there and joined with others singing the old-time familiar songs. She seemed to know all of them, and was word perfect, too.

Afterwards she said, "It was quite lovely seeing everybody so happy and enjoying themselves at last, and knowing that that ghastly war is really over."

During her stay at Badminton she had got to know most of the people and she liked them. She would be sorry to leave them, and she said so when it came to the good-byes.

"But I have got to go back to being Queen Mary," was what she said. They were very fond of her and told her that they would miss her. When they had first known that she was coming to be with them, they had been half afraid, but after they had met her they found that they could trust her implicitly; she would talk to them, and after they got over their first shyness they talked freely to her. They said that life would not be the same without her, but she promised one day to return to visit them again.

"But not because there is a war on! I hope we have had enough of that sort of thing!" she said.

She could never guess that she would return to a London that had changed so much. In her very fleeting visits to the capital, she had not had too much time to note how severe the damage had been. Marlborough House had suffered most cruelly from blast though it had never had a direct hit. It was now obvious that the raiders were trying for this when they came over, but they never actually got it. Nevertheless the doors and windows had been blown out, and she realized that it would be some time before she could return there to live.

The Ministry of Works men managed to get the first floor ready for her fairly soon, but she wanted some alterations made to the rest of it in plans that she had always had in mind, and which now would take very little more time than ordinary restoring. She was extremely good at rearranging a house, but, as she said to a friend, "You never know exactly what is wrong with a house until you have actually lived in it. Then all the bad points stick out."

For the moment the repairs had to be restricted to bare essentials, for there was such an enormous amount of rebuilding required after the blitz; there was so much for the builders to do elsewhere that one dare not ask too much. The Queen Mother knew that. If she carried out all the plans that she had in view, it would cost the country far too much, and this at a time when our resources were so weakened, and she realized that it could not be done.

"But it will be quite lovely to be home again," she said when at last the first floor had been prepared to receive her.

Everybody gets used to living in their own home, and they love it. They are accustomed to the sounds of it, the air of it, the rise of the stairs, and the feeling you get as you go up them. Queen Mary was no exception.

The men were still working on part of it when she moved in. She could take up residence, but the work would not be finished for some months. Marlborough House had never been really properly restored since the time when Edward VII and Queen Alexandra had lived there as Prince and Princess of Wales, and that was nearly half a century ago. The day when she eventually got back into what she called "my own sweet home" she was enchanted.

The difficulties that the war had brought about, the anxieties and cares, and the loss of her youngest living son, had affected her badly.

She said, "I'm not young enough for wars. No use to my country because I cannot do enough, and no real help," and she laughed about it.

She knew that she was failing in vigour, and she was getting what she called "silly little illnesses" which laid her aside for a few days, and annoyed her. She could not hold big receptions any more because they demanded too much of her, and she had not got the energy to give to them.

"It happens to everybody in time," she said: "age creeps up on us, and there we are! There really is nothing we can do about it."

Then suddenly she had a most agreeable surprise, for the ex-King, the Duke of Windsor, came home again. This was the first time they had met since he had parted with her at Windsor in 1936 – "the worse night of my life", she had called it.

It must have been, poor lady!

They had never ceased to correspond, but she had never been able to understand his disloyalty to the crown, to which she was so utterly loyal always. On 10th October 1945 he came to England and he visited his mother. She was then in her seventy-eighth year.

In her diary she wrote:

> At 4 David arrived by 'plane from Paris, on a visit to see me. I had not seen him for nearly nine years. It was a great joy to meet him again, and he looked very well. Bertie came to dinner to meet him ...

That must have been great joy for her.

She had never thought that she would see David again, and, of course, nobody knows how that dinner party went off, for undoubtedly the ex-King had submitted his unfortunate brother to the most dreadful strain of being King, the one son who had never been strong.

"Born before his time, what could you expect?" Mrs Bill once asked me rhetorically, and she had got something there.

There had been no suggestion of the Duchess of Windsor coming over with him, and the Duke did not suggest it for the Queen Mother would never have consented to that. She was not alone in that among members of the Royal Family.

Afterwards, when talking to her ladies, she said she thought her son looked well, far better than she would have expected and he was still surprisingly young-looking for his years (he was then fifty-one). She rather thought that he would never age.

She must have enjoyed the meeting enormously for it was a reunion that she had never expected; in fact she had been quite sure that she would never see her eldest son again, and then this happiness suddenly entered her world.

The brothers and their mother talked of the Duke of Kent, of whom David in particular had been so fond. Their Queen Mother was happy to let her sons talk. She thought David was in some ways wiser, less inflexible. At moments he looked sad, and she gathered that life had not been too easy, and he had had time to repent of what had happened, possibly. But every man chooses his own life, and has to abide by his choice, as she knew.

Now the little York Princesses were growing up, and already there was a lot of talk about whom Princess Elizabeth would marry. In her lay the future of the throne. In 1947 she was seeing quite a lot of young Prince Philip of Greece, Earl Mountbatten's nephew, and a very good-looking young man. The nation was eager for a love match, but nothing could happen for the moment, for the dust of war and its aftermath had hardly cleared when the Royal Family were required to tour South Africa under a long-standing pledge. The King and Queen and their two daughters were to leave the country aboard the battleship *Vanguard* at the end of January, and the date was well chosen, for the most frightful wintry weather set in as they left. It was colder than I had known it for years, and we all envied their going out into the sunshine.

When they returned the following July the blizzards, the snow and the fuel crisis were memories.

To the young Princess the long separation from Prince Philip was more painful that she admitted. For it was quite true what people around the Court were whispering; the young people were in love.

Going away until July might just as well have been for ever so far as the heir to the throne was concerned. The royal party were seen off by Queen Mary at Portsmouth. There was a fairly rough sea at the time, and neither Queen Elizabeth nor her daughters – unlike the King – could admit to being good sailors, so they hated leaving home all the more and they must have started off with real apprehension in their hearts. And one could imagine that Princess Elizabeth, who would celebrate her twenty-first birthday out there, was miserable indeed. It was four days before the weather cleared and *Vanguard* turned into calmer waters, and they were wretchedly seasick.

They made the most brilliant success of that tour. In the May of that year Queen Mary reached her eightieth birthday. She very much disliked old age, because she said that it was so insistent and so limiting, which is true. She could now do so few of the things that she wanted to do. She came from a long-lived family, and she gave a special birthday party at Marlborough House. For this she wore a pink dress which was heavily beaded, a style of dress which suited her so well, and she looked quite radiant.

She had never tried to follow the fashions of the day, but still wore dresses that she herself liked, always much the same design and cut.

She was thankful that the war was over, and that the King and Queen were doing so well in South Africa. "Our family," she said, "has a special genius for these big tours, it seems, and that makes everybody happy."

News of the tour was brought every day to the Queen Mother. She was particularly pleased when 'Lilibet' came of age, and broadcast a very good birthday speech from Cape Town to the five hundred million people of the British Empire and Commonwealth. South Africa gave her some of the most remarkable diamonds as their gift. Her grandmother was enchanted for her.

If anyone had thought that the six months' parting would come between the young people, they were wrong. They wrote regularly to each other all the time, and when the Royal Family returned home Prince Philip was one of the first callers at Buckingham Palace.

As was promised before they had started on the tour, the King announced their engagement almost immediately. Undoubtedly nothing thrilled a romantically-minded country more than a royal romance. England fell in love with Elizabeth and Philip.

The wedding was planned for 20th November 1947 – possibly not the best month, but the royals seem to be fond of winter for their weddings. For instance, the late Duke of Kent had been married in November 1934 and his older brother Henry, the Duke of Gloucester, in November, 1935 in the chapel at Buckingham Palace (for at the time King George V was desperately ill, and the ceremony, which had been originally planned for the Abbey, of course, was called off, and the Duke and his Scottish bride were married quietly).

It was said that Princess Elizabeth's wedding dress cost two thousand pounds, and it was radiantly lovely, I must say. The Queen Mother, who had always been the most generous of women, gave the young Princess some of her own jewellery, a most wonderful diamond set which she had received for her own marriage, and something that she had always valued enormously.

England was in just the right mood for romance. This was a love match we knew, and not one of what we had called Queen Victoria's 'thought-out' marriages made for official reasons.

The weather was not too good, and some of the people had been waiting all night, with busy little men rushing to and fro pushing trays of hot tea and coffee and hot pies and sausage rolls.

When the morning dawned there was only a very slight fog here and there, nothing to worry about, and nothing like as bad as it had been for Princess Marina's marriage. It cleared a little, later on. And in the afternoon when the young couple left for their honeymoon (going to Lord Mountbatten's home in the country), the sun actually shone brightly for them.

There had been such radiant autumnal weather until now, that the sun flashing out cheered us and had come, we said, to wish the happy couple joy.

Then something most unfortunate happened. They had arranged to take a house near Windlesham which was now being prepared for their reception. One night (nobody knew how it happened) it was burnt down. It was a horrible thing to happen when they were on their honeymoon. They had no home, nowhere to go, and in the end the Prince announced that they would be "living with the in-laws in Buck House".

I am sure they were distressed over this, and Queen Mary was intensely worried, for she said that all young people starting their lives together ought to have a home of their own. But, for now, the flat in the palace had to be sufficient, and a year later this was where their first child arrived. Nobody had had a baby and an heir to the throne, in the palace, since Queen Victoria. The news of the coming babe in November 1948 seemed to glamorize the winter. I am sure that Queen Mary knitted for it.

I was working on a newspaper and was one of the reporters there at the time. We all felt sure that it would be a boy, which he was, and he was named Prince Charles, which was rather surprising. I would not have said that the 'Charleses' were the luckiest of our kings, though it was high time that we got away from the heavy steady names Victoria had chosen. This little boy was baptized Charles Philip Arthur George and had a horde of noble godparents.

From the first Queen Mary had been convinced that her first great-grandchild would be a boy, and, perhaps because of the thrill of his arrival nobody seemed to notice that the King was not at all well.

It now transpired that he had had a bad leg for some time, which was constantly troubling him, and gave him quite a lot of pain. It was thrombosis. At the last minute he could not go to Sandringham for Christmas, a bitter disappointment, for he loved Norfolk, and hated breaking a custom which so far he had never failed in fulfilling. Surgeons operated on the leg, and, although they seemed at first to be pessimistic about the success of it (for it is quite a serious operation) in the end it was a surprising success.

The health of the King had always worried Mrs Bill, and, although she would not admit it, his mother, too. She had been desperately anxious over this operation. Once upon a time she had been able to accept life as it came, but she was tiring now. Growing older, she admitted. "Things worry me much more. It is so silly, for everybody does their best, and yet I get upset." She had a bad attack of sciatica that winter, which can be desperately painful, though she treated it lightly, and in letters to her friends wrote of it as being "very hampering" and "rather painful at times", which was putting it lightly.

Princess Elizabeth's second baby was due in August 1950, and came late. By now Princess Elizabeth and her husband had moved into Clarence House, which the new occupants liked very much. August was an inconvenient month because the Royal Family usually holidayed in Scotland. In the end the King went on ahead alone, and two days later Queen Elizabeth went to her daughter early in the morning, for 'it' had started. The lunch editions of the *Evening News* had the headline "It's a girl!" and all went so well that two days later the Queen joined the King at Balmoral.

In the New Year there was a special service in St Paul's Cathedral initiating the Festival of Britain. The fair opened on a fine day in Battersea Park, supposed to be like the Tivoli in Copenhagen. I love that park, and the fair was to me sheer horror and always has been. It was *nothing* like the Tivoli.

Queen Mary was in a bath chair, and her small grandson took lifts sitting at her feet, which was great fun. She looked well and waved gallantly to the crowd, getting a tremendous reception, but I thought much of the old buoyancy had gone.

We had of course come to the time when that very gay laugh of hers had disappeared; it was a lovely laugh, and now she was ageing very much indeed, although she still sat upright. I feel that she never recovered from the ordeal of the abdication, which was shattering for her, and from that time it did seem to us that she had gone downhill and she was now a martyr to those small maladies which attack the ageing. She hated this for she had never been really ill in her life.

In the summer of 1951 the King contracted a very heavy chest cold – said at first to have been 'influenza' – which did not clear up as it should have done. At first nobody was anxious; it had been a difficult summer and everybody was getting a cold. Never strong, he could not shake it off as easily as other people. But he insisted on celebrating Princess Margaret's coming-of-age at Balmoral in grand style.

We were all surprised when his doctor made him return to London for a second opinion and X-ray. It was a bronchoscopy, apparently. He came down on a rush visit, and went to see his mother, who was delighted to see him again, but although the real cause of his trouble – lung cancer – was kept from her, she felt morbid and apprehensive.

The whole of England was shaken to the core when we learnt that the King's condition was extremely serious, and that he must undergo a major operation as soon as possible. There was a growth in the lung! He was not an easy patient (always delicate) and there was a fear that his speech might be affected by the operation. This was a ghastly thought for a reigning monarch.

The Queen Mother philosophized, "It is futile trying to live events before they come. It gets nobody anywhere. Live the moment, because only the moment is given to us."

Privately she was convinced that he would get through this operation and she had few qualms, but the King suddenly looked to be quite ill. It happened very quickly.

His loss of weight was noticeable, the operation could not wait, we were told. The difficulty arose because the following spring he was going on one of those big, very trying tours overseas, this time to Australasia. All arrangements had been made and the tour could not be cancelled. Princess Elizabeth would have to take his place. This meant a trousseau of special clothes for it, and there was not a lot of time in which to get them.

Queen Mary was calm. She had been through so many agonies in her life, and now this had come out of the blue; eventually the truth could not be kept from her. The malignant growth was moving fast.

Until this hour I do not believe that most of us realized how deeply fond of the King we had become, he had been so brave. He stepped into a gap, which he must have hated doing, and he had done every possible thing that he could for the country, and had been quite wonderful during the war. He was the King whom everybody loved, and not for the world did we want anything to happen to him.

The country received this ghastly piece of bad news with grief and dismay.

The Royal Family were part of our personal lives, and we shared their troubles and their joys, it seemed, and were so grateful to this brave young man who had taken over when his elder brother had failed us.

Special nurses were selected, four of them to be with him day and night, and the prayers of the nation were given him.

The Queen Mother tried to endow her son with some of her own courage, for he was dreadfully worried about having to cancel the overseas tour. She now knew that the affected lung would have to be removed, and there was very real danger, but she did everything that she could to help little Queen Elizabeth and the grandchildren.

The person now worked almost to death was Princess Elizabeth who was taking on the royal tour. She had to get all the right clothes for it. She went from one fitting to the next. Maybe the fact that she had so much to do did help her a little, for she was dreadfully distressed about it all.

The Queen Mother sadly but indomitably braced herself to meet this latest in a chain of personal disasters which seemed to have dogged her from childhood.

13

Suddenly, at Home...

The operation on King George VI was arranged to take place on Sunday 23rd September at Buckingham Palace. A complete operating theatre had been set up there, with everything that was needed.

On the morning of the day, in the presence of waiting crowds, three carriages drove out of the palace gates. The Queen and her two daughters went to church to take Communion and to pray for the life of the King. They tried hard to conceal their desperate anxiety.

The Queen Mother was distressed not to be with them, but her doctors advised her to stay indoors at Marlborough House.

The royal party returned to the palace as quietly as they had left it, without any applause, because we were afraid of disturbing the invalid. We prayed that they were comforted. The Queen waved to us.

The operation began very early that day, and it took much longer than the surgeons had predicted. Those waiting had become anxious, and when the bulletin was posted outside the palace, telling us it was safely over, and the King was doing well, nobody dared cheer! The crowd gasped with relief. (We had feared he might die, for he had looked to be so dreadfully ill.)

The Queen was able to speak to him for the first time two days later. He was in the care of the four specially selected nurses, and we felt everything now rested with them. Recovery could not be hurried in any way we knew, but he *was* making progress.

He got better far sooner than they had predicted, and, owing to the brilliance of his surgeons, his speech was not affected. I remember three weeks later I went to a theatre and the Queen was there and, with her, the four nurses, 'taken out for a treat' I imagined. The Queen thought that they had earned a treat, but I do not suppose for a single moment that they expected to get the reception that they were given, for they came in quietly, and when they were recognized they got the most rousing cheer that I have ever heard in a theatre. We owed them a lot, we felt.

At first the King could speak very little, but the fact that he could speak at all was the thing that mattered and we were all reassured. Now his main private worry was if he could get well enough to spend Christmas down at Sandringham, for as yet the doctors would not commit themselves to this.

"You see, I am a Norfolk man," he told the doctors, "and I *want* to go home."

Once he got over the first shock and the extreme fatigue which accompanied this particular operation, he progressed exceedingly well, far better than anyone had thought that he could. He was more himself than he had been for years, but he was painfully thin.

Mrs Bill told me, "He will always do what he is told. I never had to tell him anything twice. The others would argue. Prince Harry was obstinate, but Prince Albert was no trouble to anybody" – and she said it with real affection.

He did get down to Sandringham for Christmas. At Liverpool Street station he received a magnificent welcome. He embarked on the royal train, his mother with him.

"Lovely to be going home," she said.

Admittedly when they got to Wolferton station he seemed to be very tired. There was the station-master waiting to greet the King with a big smile and in his best uniform, also with holly in his cap, as was seasonable. He had a radiant smile for the King. Norfolk rejoiced that he was better, and he said a bit of Sandringham air would do everything for him.

I think they had possibly thought that they would never see him again, but Queen Mary felt sure Sandringham would help him.

"It's like old times," she said, "and here we are for a merry Christmas again, in the good old way."

She had been very anxious for him, although she was always sure that he would get over it. But now age was worrying her. She fell asleep so easily, having no idea that she was doing it, and then was ashamed when she woke up and found that she *had* done it. She could not walk about as she had done and she got tired so very quickly.

But she was still able to meet old friends, and to go about in her bath-chair, even if it was, as she said, "something of a come-down".

She stayed in her room most of the time, which was unlike her old self, for she had loved being out and about and doing things, and visiting people that she knew. On 15th January she returned to Marlborough House. Her doctors were not too happy about her being at Sandringham, for they thought that Norfolk was rather cold for her. She had an abiding faith in their knowledge, and in the way that they had helped the King. Of course, nobody could tell if the King's trouble would return, the surgeons always hoped not, but for the moment he only had to put on weight, and be himself again. One had to live for the moment with these cases.

The hour came when Princess Elizabeth and Prince Philip would be starting on their Commonwealth tour, which she was carrying out in her father's place. She would be almost glad to go, for she was sick of eternal tryings-on, and for ever choosing clothes. The family came back to London to see her off, and then would return to Norfolk to finish their holiday.

Queen Mary could not go with them to the airport, for she had had a chill and the doctors would not let her risk it. "I am very annoyed with them," she said.

She hated not being 'in' on everything that was going on, though, when she thought about it she knew that her old strength was not here any more, and she tired almost instantly. She was also a trifle bewildered by the quick pace at which modern life proceeded, and she excused her dislike by saying,

"Oh well, I suppose we all get old, and there *are* dreadful liabilities attached to it."

The King and Queen with their younger daughters saw their older daughter and her husband off on this great tour. The King walked out on to the tarmac with them, which was a very good sign. It was one of those very chilly winter days, with glowering skies, and quite plainly the English winter was not over. They went into the plane to say their good-byes, and when they came down again, it seemed that they all looked happy, and the King was considerably better than he had been, although his appearance shocked many people. Sandringham had done him good, he always said there was no place like it, loved wandering round the stables and the yard at the back, and then down by the lake and round to the house where he had been born.

"I was something of a surprise packet" was the way that he put it when in a good mood, "and what they would have done if I had arrived before the Home Secretary I simply cannot think. Queen Victoria would *not* have been amused" – and he laughed about it.

He had great charm.

Christmas had come and gone – the King's last Christmas – with the usual visit of the carollers on Christmas Eve, singing in the hall and welcomed with enthusiasm. It would not have been a Sandringham Christmas without them. There was a service at the little church at the far end of the park, such a sweet little church, he had always loved it.

As the Royal Family always said, Sandringham was home. Windsor Castle was never in quite the same position for them, and, of course, nobody could ever get really fond of Buckingham Palace, which was, as one of the young princes had once said, "a good place to get lost in, for you would never find yourself again!"

He had been determined to go to London airport to see his daughter off. He and the Queen and Princess Margaret had come down the steps of the 'plane again, having said their farewells. It was perhaps a good thing that they did not know it was good-bye for ever for the King, for they were a devoted family.

So he had waved his daughter away, and the 'plane had travelled fast and he watched it until it was a blur in the sky, and then suddenly it had gone. He turned back to the car and drove down to Sandringham again.

Perhaps it was a long way for him.

Perhaps he would have been wiser to spend another night at the palace, but none of the Royal Family was really very fond of the palace, and all of them adored Sandringham.

They said that he did not seem to be over-tired, for he had dozed part of the way and seemed far less weary than anybody had thought that he would be.

He rested at home for a time, and he ate a good dinner that night, and afterwards he and the Queen sat listening to Princess Margaret playing the piano for him, something that he loved. It was a quiet evening, in their own home.

It had distressed Queen Mary very much that she simply was not well enough to go down to the airport to see 'Lilibet' off, as she wanted to do. She would have gone if it had been possible, but now she was constantly 'not very well', with no real name to the illness, but just 'off colour'. She watched the take-off on television, of course, which although it was not quite the same thing, was a most useful substitute, and one did see things clearly, and with no crowds.

They had said good-bye the day before, and she had telephoned on the morning of departure, for she adored her grand-daughter, and wished her well. Later she rang up Sandringham to know how the King felt after the journey. It had been a big effort, almost the first time that he had appeared in public again, and she did hope that he was not worn out.

Strangely enough, he was quite well, he said, and felt better for having made the effort.

His mother went to bed that night quite happily for she had

been worried over his making this effort. But, as she always said, it was no good getting worried over whatever lay ahead for one. Now was the time that mattered, and apparently he had seen 'Lilibet' off, and felt not at all too badly. He had slept most of the way down, and was glad to be back at home.

She felt contented that her son was now returning to his normal life, and one must hope that the trouble would never recur. His doctors were amazingly hopeful. They had done an extensive job, it had taken longer than expected, but they *had* done it well.

She thought of the young couple flying out to a new country. In fact they had landed in Kenya at the start of the tour and were having the most wonderful time, seeing by moonlight a water hole where wild animals came down to drink. It was a new world to the Princess, and she was quite enchanted by it.

She will enjoy the tour, really, her grandmother mused, and remembered how she had enjoyed those hideously tiring tours, but they had had a lot to do, and much that had made her very happy. She thought of the Durbar in India, and that very hot dress that she had brought with her, never thinking that it could be quite so hot as it was. Nowadays she sometimes wondered how she had ever done everything that she had done, but, then, she had had the strength to carry on, and now perhaps she was too old. But, looking back on life is very different from living it, was what she told herself.

She awoke next morning feeling better, rose and dressed, and was attending to her mail with her secretary when she was told that Lady Cynthia Colville, a woman-of-the-bedchamber, had asked for permission to speak with Her Majesty. This was unusual at this hour. Instinctively Queen Mary must have known that it was something important; she immediately suspected that something was wrong.

"I will see her," she said.

The secretary disappeared and Lady Cynthia entered, curtseyed, and paused, looking at the Queen (as she expressed it later) rather differently from usual. There was something about her manner that gave the message she must be shuddering to disclose. The Queen recognized the situation very quickly, and she asked in a brave voice that did not falter, "Is it the King?"

She paused then for intuitively she knew before Lady Cynthia answered her that she was right – it *was* the King.

The message had come from Sandringham to Marlborough House, and the details were shattering.

The previous evening the King had had a quiet time, listening to his younger daughter's music, and then he had gone to bed at the usual hour. He had said that he was surprised that he was not too tired, all of which showed that he was rapidly getting better.

They were also surprised that he was not exhausted, for he had done quite a lot when he was in London, and had seen his specialist, who had been pleased with him. Then he had eaten a good dinner, and appeared to be quite himself. He was getting so much better and the little Queen was feeling far happier about him.

But next morning, at the set hour, his valet brought him his early morning tea, and spoke to him. But the King did not stir. Discreetly the valet drew the blinds, and then, going over to the bed, put out a gentle hand to awaken his master. It was then that he thought His Majesty was lying extremely still, and he could not hear him breathing.

He was dead!

I cannot imagine the panic of the next few minutes, when the man was quite sure of this, and had to tell the lady-in-waiting to inform the Queen. Nobody had expected this. There had been no warning from his doctors; in fact, they had been reassured that, as he was doing now, he would put on weight and get better still.

Queen Mary herself had felt that the first danger was over. She had realized, only too well, that there was the horror that the cancer might return, though the doctors had removed everything malignant that they could. The fact that he could go down to Sandringham had made his mother feel that he must be really better now.

She stared at the lady-in-waiting who brought her the

numbing news as though she were a complete stranger, and someone she had never seen before. She stared with an awful silence.

Then she said, "What will Lilibet do?"

She was the woman who always thought for others first, and not of herself.

Prince Philip had to break the dreadful news to the Princess, now Queen Elizabeth II. She took it very badly, because it was something that was so entirely unexpected. Three months back they had almost despaired of him, but now, when he was almost well again (it was merely a matter of putting on more weight) she could not believe that this was true.

They made all necessary emergency arrangements to return home as quickly as possible. It was appalling to have to cancel the entire tour, and with decorated cities waiting to receive them, but death can be abrupt. Death answers all arguments.

The poor new young Queen was completely shattered by the news that she had never thought to be possible. She had believed (as did the others) that now the King was so far away from that operation that he would be getting better all the time. In the last few weeks he had been far more himself, and going down to Sandringham had seemed to help him.

The whole nation and Commonwealth were paralysed by the news.

I got it before others knew, for I was working on a newspaper at the time, and I admit that it *horrified* me. At first I could not believe it.

The new Queen left Kenya for Britain that night. At London Airport next day she walked down the gangway of the 'plane in black, alone and looking terribly slim. It was plain that she had been crying very much, her eyes were quite pathetic, but she herself was bravely calm. How they teach the Royal Family this courage I do not know, but they manage it somehow.

Four Ministers of the Crown were standing awaiting their

Queen. Her grandmother saw the arrival on television. She always said that, in some ways television was a tremendous boon, but in others it made one dreadfully sad, and she must have felt that when the very young girl, who had left us but a few hours previously, returned fatherless to her country.

This King had been the most devoted father; he was a family man, one who had never wanted to be King but had bravely stepped into the breach when his elder brother left the country for ever.

The only thing that relieved Queen Mary's grief was the thought that her son had died in his favourite home, close to the house where he had been born. Somehow she felt that he would have wished that.

Two kings had died at Sandringham, and she had seen her first love, Prince Albert Victor, die in his mother's arms, a terrible experience for a young girl. She was shocked now into speechlessness for a time. She simply could not believe that it had happened, but Bertie had died without suffering and one should be grateful for that.

The body of George VI lay in state as his father had done in the little church of Sandringham, with his own keepers keeping guard over him. Then it was brought to London with a downpour falling, and it seemed that the heart of London was shattered by this tragedy, so terribly, terribly unexpected.

14

Brave to the End

The doctors tried to persuade Queen Mary not to attend the funeral, for she was still suffering badly from shock. But she wanted to do what she felt to be a duty.

"He was my son," she said, "and my King, and I have followed too many. I must be with him and I have every right to be."

The doctors decided that it would only upset her more if they tried to lay down the law, and for the moment they left the question open. She was a very adamant woman like her mother-in-law, Queen Alexandra, and if she meant to go, she would go.

She had a long talk with the new Queen, and this helped both of them. Possibly Queen Mary did not realize how great the shock had been to her when she had said that she would go to the funeral. But she found that shock was taking it out of her and she began to fret. She still was sure that she would go to the funeral, but then she started to waver. That was when the protesting doctors stepped in.

She knew she was now feeling very much older than she had done before. She felt ill, she became unsure of her capacity to go to the funeral, and at length she did what the doctors had asked of her.

"Perhaps they know best," she said, but she would have felt that in some way she was failing her son.

I think this loss aged her terribly, because it came as a bolt from the blue. The shock affected her already failing memory. When talking she would suddenly forget what it was she had been going to say, and was ashamed of herself.

"It is so muddling to forget," she said sadly, and there was little that could be done to help her.

When she got over the first shock she improved and could attend to her letters, a task she had always liked doing, and thought that she ought to do herself. It was hard work, of course, for she received a very big post, but she liked reading letters, she said, and replying to them when she could.

She said, "If you are a Queen you expect to work hard. There is always something waiting for us to do."

She did not want to break the rules she abided by, and the jobs that she had always done, like answering letters. Yet she still had some good days, and these helped her.

She went to see the exhibition of Leonardo da Vinci at Burlington House, which gave her great pleasure. This was something that she had very much wanted to do and she surprised everybody by appearing there. It was like old times seeing the Queen Mother for big exhibitions had always fascinated her, she was extremely well informed about art, and she would have wished to do this more frequently.

Feeling better, she went off to Kensington Palace because she wanted to verify something about the coronation robe which had been worn by Queen Victoria at her own coronation, and which she thought might be useful to 'Lilibet'. She knew that there had been certain points about it which would help the new Queen, who was busy over her own dress for this great occasion.

But privately she was very concerned about herself and the coming coronation. She knew the routine well: there had been her own, she had seen King Edward VII crowned before that, and her second son taking his brother's place, Prince Albert. These *are* very long and fatiguing ceremonies and she tired so quickly and it would be unthinkable if she fell asleep during the coronation. But it was possible. This dreadful habit of just dropping off to sleep worried her. What could she do?

In the end the doctors persuaded her not to go.

Time was now moving fast for her. By the end of May 1952 she had celebrated her eighty-fifth – and her last – birthday. She had recovered very much for this and actually enjoyed it. On the evening of her birthday she had written in her diary that she had enjoyed it very much indeed.

> A nice fine day, my 85th birthday and such a hectic morning, with endless flowers. My family came to see me, very nice of them, and I felt very much spoilt, and a nice day, in spite of my great age.

She spent most of that summer down at Sandringham, where she wished to be, but she had to go everywhere in the gardens in her bath-chair. She visited people near at hand whom she wanted to see, and liked that, for she was still amazingly energetic, and loved going about. But she did admit that she very quickly got worn out, when she had really done very little, and this irritated her. It seemed to be so stupid! Now the walk down to the lake that she loved, which at one time she had never even thought about twice, seemed to entail a tremendous effort which was more than she could do.

She returned to Marlborough House for the autumn, but could not do very much and disliked the fact that she did less and less.

She went back to Sandringham again for Christmas because, as she said, it would not be Christmas if she did not go there. But she got up later, and went to bed earlier, and she was constantly having what she called "little lie downs". But this time she did find Norfolk cold, and she went back to Marlborough House sooner than she had originally arranged.

I am sure that she never really got over the terrible blow of the King's death; for her it *was* the end. Usually she had had a premonition of trouble, something that had been with her all her life. On the night that Prince George had died, she suddenly said, "Something is very wrong. I feel it and yet I don't know what it is." Then an hour later the message came about the fatal air crash in Scotland.

But she had had no inkling of George VI's death. She said, "It might have been me. It *should* have been me before him. Bertie should have lived for many years."

She disliked the fact that she would not be well enough to attend 'Lilibet's' coronation in June; it would be too long for her, and the strain it entailed would be too great.

They told her that she would see it very well on television in Marlborough House, and far more comfortably. She accepted this, and liked to be kept up with the news.

Tragically, with the coronation very close indeed, she suddenly became ill again. To the outer world it was called 'a chill', anything to hide the real fact that the greatest Queen Consort we had ever had was approaching the end of the road. She had had a premonition of death, and had given express orders that if she died soon the coronation must not be postponed.

They did everything that they could for her, but at times she was not sure of herself, nor of where she was, nor of what was actually happening. They could do very little, she was too old, she lingered for a few days, with the Princess Royal always by her side.

There came the evening when the rest of the family were summoned to Marlborough House to say good-bye to her, for now the end was very near. Already she had drifted into a haze, with moments of consciousness when she recognized them and knew where she was, and then drifted off again.

The last time that she was really conscious she talked of her own end, seeking that there should be no mourning for her, for nothing like that must clash with the glory of 'Lilibet's' coronation, and she repeated this incessantly! She wanted no fuss, and no to-do, because this should be the hour of rejoicing for the new Queen of England, who was to be crowned in the Abbey.

It must have been agonizing for them, for they all were very fond of her, her kind care for them, and the tremendous comfort she had always been when in trouble. One by one they said good-bye, and on 24th March 1953 she passed into unconsciousness, and never woke up again. It was the end.

Everything that she asked was done. She had been most insistent that they must do what she wanted, and her passing must in no way interfere with the coronation.

In the very early morning, when nobody was about, a hearse came quietly into the garden of Marlborough House. The sentry on duty had expected it. This hearse took her body down to Westminster Hall, long before people were up and doing, with nothing special to attract attention to the fact that this was the greatest Queen Consort we had ever had, and they were carrying out her last orders to them.

The subsequent funeral service itself was comparatively quiet, as she had asked. She was buried at St George's, Windsor, beside her husband, as she had always asked to be, and the effigy for which she had so courageously sat was put there to her memory. Some said that it was a shame that perhaps our greatest Queen should be buried without any of the usual panoply, but this she had asked, for the coronation was so near and she did not want an elaborate state funeral to detract from it in any way. The Duke of Windsor walked behind her coffin.

I think this Queen suffered more than any of the previous ones, from the time when her engagement to Prince Albert Victor had ended with his death, and she standing by to the end. She had lived through two terrible wars knowing much of the backroom news (and at times we were very close to danger), and she had also experienced more personal unhappiness than most other Queen Consorts.

But she had known happiness, too. She and King George V were very happy together and understood one another. He was a difficult man at moments, but they had known each other from babyhood, and they did have very happy times together.

I do not know how she survived the abdication, for this was something which, as she said, she could hardly believe was true. The death of Prince George was, I am sure, a harsh blow – unexpected, like the death of George VI. Then, when that son died, she must have felt it was the end.

There was nothing that she would not have done, and did not do, for England. Mrs Bill told me that, and she knew her almost better than anybody else, the faithful nurse who brought up the children and always said: "I could trust them all, but not Prince Edward. He *was* the difficult one."

Mrs Bill told me more about Queen Mary than anyone else, and her tremendous fondness for her showed itself every time.

"She always thought for others," said Mrs Bill, and told me that one day the Queen went to see her, and they talked together on the veranda at the back of her house. The Queen thought it was draughty and said so, and, within a week, men appeared with a load of glass "to glass it in". "She did things like that," Mrs Bill said, with a deep sigh, for she was devoted to her. Perhaps that was her great secret. She always thought of others.